BUSINESS
SUCCESS
INSIDER FORMULA

BUILD A BUSINESS THAT SAVES YOU TIME AND RUNS LIKE CLOCKWORK

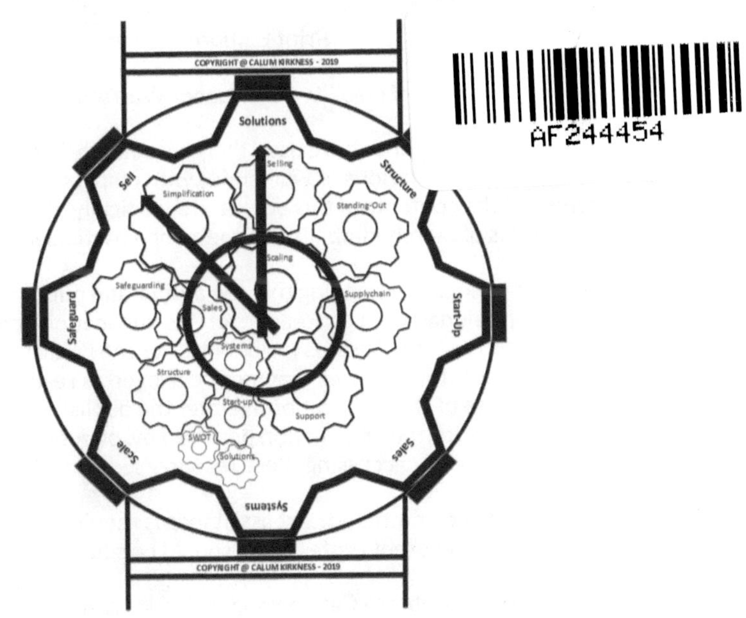

CALUM KIRKNESS

COPYRIGHT

Powerhouse Publications
94/124 London Road
Oxford
OX3 9FN

www.powerhousepublishing.com

Print Edition

Limit of Liability / Disclaimer Warranty:

British Library Cataloguing in Publication Data.
A catalogue record of this book is available from the British Library.
Cover design, editing, formatting by Oxford Literary Consultancy.

www.oxfordwriters.com

Best Way to Connect And Keep In Touch:

LinkedIn: Calum Kirkness and Business Success Insider

Facebook: Calum Kirkness and Business Success Insider

Instagram: Calum Kirkness and Business Success Insider

DEDICATION

This book is dedicated to both my late grandfathers, my father and my mother for their support, encouragement and lessons in business, property and life. Without them, this book would not have been possible.

I would also like to dedicate this book to all the people who refuse to settle for mediocrity and have the courage, strength and belief to take the enormous opportunities that are available to make a difference in the world.

ACKNOWLEDGEMENTS

There are many people who have made an impact in my life that I would like to thank. There are too many to mention individually, but there are a few who stand out as being the ones who have created a lifelong and positive lasting impression.

I would like to thank the following people for their support, guidance, inspiration and the lifelong positive impact that they have made:

- My mother, for her love and support.
- My late father, for his support and teaching me his skills and knowledge.
- Both my late grandfathers, for the lessons learned from their success in business and property.
- My close friends, for their support and encouragement.
- Finally, everyone who I have met on my journey. I have learnt something from everyone I have met, which I am grateful for.

ABOUT THE AUTHOR

CALUM KIRKNESS is a self-made serial entrepreneur as well as CEO and founder of several companies. He is an internationally-recognised and respected entrepreneur and property expert with over 30 years' experience in business and property investment and development. Calum has invested significant amounts of time and money in his own personal development, learning from some of the best in business, entrepreneurship, public speaking, property investment and development to gain the depth of knowledge and expertise that he has today.

Calum developed a passion for business, property, freedom and wealth from a very young age. After a difficult start in life, growing up with a father who was battling with alcohol addiction, financial resources were tight and home life was dysfunctional. This led Calum to realise the importance and value of money and mindset, and how having both provides freedom. He started working and began his first entrepreneurial endeavours when he was just 12 years old.

Calum was always good with money and a good saver, and learned the power of the compound effect from seeing his savings grow from the high interest being earned during his teenage years in the 1980s.

By the age of 19, Calum had started his first construction company and it wasn't long before he started employing people and leased a workshop facility. He was working very long hours and dedicating his whole life to the business, which he would later find out would be a big mistake.

By the age of 23, he had saved enough funds to buy his first plot of development land and began his property development journey and building up his own property portfolio. In the early years, Calum took a very hands-on hard-work approach to achieving success. This led him to learn the lesson that exchanging your time for money is not a scalable model or good for your health – and certainly not a route to achieving success and freedom.

At the age of 36, Calum bought another building company and amalgamated it into his existing business. This almost doubled the size of the business overnight – which solved some problems but created others. Calum soon discovered that there were still some key things missing from his business and business knowledge. This led him to continue to invest significant amounts of time and money into his personal development to obtain the knowledge that successful people had used to achieve their success. He now shares this information in this book to help those looking to build their dream business that will enable them to live the life of their dreams on their own terms.

Calum now focuses much of his time on developing Business Success Insider and Property Success Insider into international investment, development, educational and training companies, with ambitious plans. Calum is also currently working on several exciting projects, which are in the early stages of development, and will be multi-million-pound projects if they go ahead.

CONTENTS

INTRODUCTION

It is a great idea to make BUSINESS your BUSINESS – and there is no better time than now. If you wish to build a business that saves you time and runs like clockwork, you have the right book in your hands to enable you to THRIVE in your business and personal life rather than just SURVIVE.

Business Success Insider Formula is the book that I wish I had had at the beginning of my journey. Had I had this book when I was 15, I am sure that I could have been a billionaire today. It is still one of my goals that I am working on, however what is more important than being a millionaire or billionaire in monetary terms is becoming someone who has positively changed millions or billions of lives. No one will remember you from having millions or billions of pounds in the bank, but you will be remembered if you have changed millions or billions of lives.

A book is one of the ways that many people can be reached at a relatively-low cost, which is one of my inspirations for writing this book and getting the information out there and available to help people.

The earlier in life we obtain the right information and start to work towards our goals and build our dreams, the better it is. The bigger the contribution and value we provide, the greater the rewards that we will receive.

After years of working hard on building up my businesses in the early part of my journey, which was much more stressful and took up much more of my time than I thought, I was achieving a certain level of success. However, I was trapped working in my businesses rather than working on them and unable to reach the level of time and financial freedom that I was hoping for. I consequently ended up stressed, frustrated and burnt out on more than one occasion. This is a situation that many business owners find themselves in. Some fail, some go back to employment and some continue to be trapped working in their business just managing to survive. But it doesn't have to be this way. There are a small number of people who understand the insider secrets, but keep them to themselves or charge a lot to share them. I am sharing with you as much insider information and knowledge as is possible in a book to enable you to build a successful business that frees up your time and has the potential to provide you with the financial freedom to live life on your own terms.

Since I was young, I could see a few people living the sort of life that I wanted to achieve and reach the heights of success that I desired. They all had their own businesses, so I knew it was possible, which gave me the courage and determination to keep going. I could also see and understand that it would never be possible as an employee or even as a self-employed person. After working for a few years as a self-employed person, I knew that I didn't have all the right answers figured out yet to build the business that I so desired, so I decided to invest in my personal development and go to some business and mindset training events and hire millionaire and billionaire coaches and mentors to help me. What I discovered is that I was doing some of the right things well, but I was missing a few key components and knowledge that would make all the difference and create the results that I wanted. If we continue to take the same actions over and over again, hoping to achieve a different result, this is what Einstein referred to as Insanity.

Having an open, growth mindset is key to discovering the answers that we require. We know what we know, we know what we don't know, but we don't know what we don't know. The latter forms the biggest percentage of information.

Reading books is one of the best ways to learn new information and is a habit that 90% of all successful people have and continue with, so you have made a great decision and investment in your time and money in getting and reading this book. Warren Buffett, who is one of the world's greatest investors, says that the best investment that you can ever make is in yourself.

I have invested a six-figure sum in my own personal development to learn from some of the best and I would like to give everyone who is interested access to the most valuable information that I have learned to build a business that has the potential to run like clockwork and free up your time to be living the lifestyle that you have always wanted.

Personal development and business have the potential to make you a fortune, whereas employment and self-employment will make you a living.

In business, 20% of actions create 80% of the results. The key is to learn, understand, discover and focus on what the 20% of actions required are to create the 80% of the results. Those who are working hard tend to be concentrating on the 80% that bring the 20% of results, whilst those who are working smart are working on the 20% that bring in 80% of the results.

We all have six basic human needs and having your own business is a great way to meet them. One of these needs is contribution. This is one of the things that inspires me to write books today to contribute and give back by sharing my knowledge and experience to provide others with a better chance of living a better life. Success comes from creating more content than we consume and contributing more than we take. Writing a book is a great way to create content that can be read by millions and a great way to contribute to the world by sharing valuable information at a low cost. A book also positions you as an expert in your field and helps build a brand, which I would encourage you to do also. I share more on these topics throughout the book.

Most very successful people did not start out to make a lot of money, they set out to make a difference. They had a dream, a vision and the courage to follow their intuition. The reward they received reflects the difference that they have made, or continue to make, to people's lives and the world. Think of Mark Zuckerburg at Facebook, Jeff Bezos at Amazon, Bill Gates at Microsoft, Steve Jobs at Apple, Oprah Winfrey with her own TV Network, and J K Rowling, author of Harry Potter books, as a few recent examples of successful people and businesses. They all started from humble beginnings in a spare room or garage, some of them with nothing, and went on to build huge businesses and success around what they were passionate about and reaped huge rewards, which I'm sure have exceeded their wildest expectations. It is also interesting how many of them dropped out of college to follow their dreams and continued despite getting knocked back.

Business is all about solving a problem or filling a need for as many people as possible. The bigger the problem that you can solve, or the bigger the need that you can fill for the most amount of people, the bigger your reward will be.

It is time for you to STOP SURVIVING and START THRIVING. You have it within you to do that.

In this book, I will be sharing with you the steps that you can take to create and build your dream business that, when followed, will allow your business to operate like a quality Swiss time piece, and give you the potential to have the time and financial freedom to live life on your terms,. This is something that cannot be achieved from being employed, self-employed or even having your own business, if a few of the key component parts or knowledge are missing. You will find a lot of the business knowledge and life lessons that you require in order to be successful in this book.

There are millions of people around the world who have chosen the so-called "safe" traditional route of education, going to college, getting a job, working their way up the career ladder, buying a house, having the nice car and goods, paying into a pension and doing all the things that society says we should do to feel successful, who are feeling stuck, unhappy, unfulfilled and working for the weekends or holidays. No one ever became financially free working as an employee and many people are now finding themselves having to work in to their late seventies just to survive, or spend their retirement living in poverty. The traditional route is a broken model, which I guess you already know and is why you are reading this book.

> *"When we are too afraid to risk anything, we sooner or later*
> *come to realise that we have risked everything by default in*
> *the process. This can be our transformation point that is the*
> *trigger to catapulting us to reach incredible levels of success."*
> **– Calum Kirkness**

> *"It is not essential to have money to make money. What you*
> *need, and is essential, is having resourcefulness*
> *and belief in yourself."*
> **– Calum Kirkness**

Entrepreneurship is the route where you can earn more than a doctor or consultant without having any formal qualifications. Think of all the years of expenses and lost income achieving a university degree to end up being in debt before you even start earning an income. It is much better to have a nice bank balance, a nice lifestyle and the opportunity to contribute to the world than merely having a nice title.

The good news is that there has never been a better time in history when there were more opportunities to start a business and be successful than there are today. Technology has made starting a business easier and more accessible to more people than ever before, yet the rapid speed of progress that was supposed to have made our lives easier and more comfortable, has also created more problems than we have ever had before. With change comes opportunity and this is fantastic news if you are an entrepreneur with a solution-focused mind. Opportunities are everywhere, but they do come and go and have a shelf life. It is important to grab them when they come along and capitalise on them when the timing is right, and let them go when they reach their expiry date. I will go into more detail on this in the book.

I believe that everyone has a level of untapped genius and potential inside them. These are gifts in the form of exceptional talents, skills, passions. Our purpose in life is to find these gifts and serve them to the world. This is our contribution and gift back, which we will be rewarded for in equal or greater measure.

There are many more budding entrepreneurs in existence with great potential, who are being held back from starting their businesses due to their fears and limiting beliefs. A large part of our success in life will come down to the people we were around when we were young and surround ourselves with now, which we will have a look at in detail later in the book. Our environment where we work, rest and play is very important as to whether we will achieve success in life.

An important part of the entrepreneur journey, and one which should be explored right at the start, is finding your true gifts to thrive in business. Figuring out your true gifts requires soul-searching by taking a close look at your values, what makes you feel energised and come alive, and how you best interact with others.

We all get into business with the aim to win. The key to winning in any business is to align with your true nature and do something that you are passionate about. Entrepreneurship can satisfy many of our basic human needs such as growth, variety and contribution. Becoming an entrepreneur and starting your own business is a life-changing experience and journey that is not for everyone, but I doubt if anyone who has embarked on the journey has ever truly regretted it.

We always have a choice in life: we can either use our skills, talents and passions to work on our dreams or live in victim mode and feel too afraid and fearful to work on and follow them. If we don't work on our own dreams, someone else will employ us to work on theirs. A ship is safe in the harbour, but that is not what it is designed for. The good news is that you are the captain of your ship and you get to decide and chart the journey ahead. There will be rough periods and we can never adjust the direction of the wind, but we can always adjust the direction of the sails.

Monetising your knowledge, experience, skills and talents through a business can provide great benefits to you, your customers and the wider world. Selling is serving and if you have a solution that can help others solve a problem or fill a need, then I believe that you have a duty to develop and offer it. To not offer your unique gifts to the world is a selfish and unhealthy act, which usually ends up later becoming regret.

I hope that you enjoy reading this book and get lots of valuable knowledge, information and tips to help you identify your unique gifts and unleash them on the world.

"Believe in yourself and believe in your dreams."
– Calum Kirkness

"In order to survive in today's fast-changing world, having the
ability to adapt is much more important
than having strength."
– Calum Kirkness

Be warned: this book goes deep. I would encourage you to read the book from cover to cover, without skipping any sections and you will see how each section links with the others and how each individual part is important in understanding the whole process to building a business that has the potential to run like clockwork. Missing just one or two key parts can have a massive impact on your overall results and success. It may be difficult and a bit uncomfortable to grasp the first time around, but once you have read the book a second time, the picture will become clearer and much easier to understand. The more you focus on a strategy and area, the easier and quicker you can build your expertise and success.

If we wait until we are fully ready, we will never start and most likely be too late. The key is to get the 20% ready that will brings in 80% of the results and launch immediately. The other 80% can be discovered along the way. Think of Apple and the difference between the first version of the iPhone and the current version. Your customers are unlikely to even notice that you weren't ready.

The opportunity for you to make serious amounts of money and build wealth from investing in and building your own business in the UK, international and global markets is huge; it is real, and the opportunities and possibilities are endless. It is available right now and it all begins with you raising your awareness and acting on these ideas and this information.

CHAPTER 1

HOW MY BUSINESS AND PROPERTY JOURNEY BEGAN AND DEVELOPED

I was born with business, property and entrepreneurial spirit in my DNA! My grandfather had his own building and property development company... my father followed in his father's footsteps... and then I followed the same path. Talk about history repeating itself! On my mother's side, my grandparents also ran their own business, which was a mini-market, fuel station, garage and private transport business. In my early years, I would spend most of my summer holidays with my grandparents experiencing their business operations.

It is said that what we are exposed to in the first seven years of our life shapes to a large extent who we become and how we live the rest of our life! Some say it dictates 95% of what we do in our adult lives, which I do believe is true. However, once we are aware of this, there are things we can do to increase our knowledge and awareness, get rid of our limiting beliefs, and change our habits to achieve the levels of success that we desire.

Since I could first see, hear and walk, I was exposed to the retail, service, construction sectors of business and also property investment and development models. I have fond memories of exploring my way around building sites and being with my grandparents in their shop and garage business in my early years, watching and listening to what was being done to develop the sites and properties into what would become much-needed homes and watching customers shop for groceries and have their cars repaired, etc.

My grandfather was a carpenter who started his own building company shortly after the Second World War. There was a shortage of accommodation and money at the time and he spotted an opportunity to provide a valuable solution to a big problem. After the War was over, the military started selling off the redundant accommodation buildings (the buildings were sold separately to the land). The buildings were large (long) timber frame and timber clad, and my grandfather's vision and solution was to buy these timber buildings, carve them up into house-size sections and transport and re-construct them on the customer's land to create a new family home.

Me and my father   Me and my grandfather

Once all the timber-frame, war-time buildings purchased by my grandfather had been converted into homes, he used the rewards from the venture to fund the next opportunity. By this time, the country was beginning to recover, people were starting to have money and were looking for new traditional-build family houses. He used the capital that he had accumulated to purchase green-field development land in the main town and in the village where he lived (and where I was brought up). He then concentrated on building three-bedroom detached bungalows to sell. He continued with this strategy for many years with success until he retired. He also carried out building and construction work for customers to build bespoke one-off houses, and commercial and farm buildings, etc. My grandfather had a great vision and ability to spot opportunities as well as the courage to take risks. He became wealthy in the process. Looking back, I feel he made one big mistake, which was not keeping some of the properties for himself to provide a recurring passive income stream in his retirement and to continue to build wealth through capital appreciation. His wealth would decline in retirement: I am sure he had investments in shares and pension funds, etc, but it's a good example of how it is not always wise to rely solely on them.

"Grab opportunities when they come along."
– Calum Kirkness

*"All opportunities have a shelf life. Avoid pursuing
opportunities after their sell-by date."*
– Calum Kirkness

"Look for solutions to problems and offer them."
– Calum Kirkness

*"The bigger the problem that you can solve,
the bigger the reward."*
– Calum Kirkness

*"Trust your vision for the future: believe in the magic of your
intuition and go for it!"*
– Calum Kirkness

When my father left school at the age of 15, he joined his father's construction, building and property development company as a carpenter and joiner. He worked hard and learned a wide range of construction skills. He was popular and well-respected with the workforce and the community, but due to family dynamics he left and went his own way, starting his own building company when my grandfather retired. My father had the skills and the work ethic, but he didn't have the same vision and level of business acumen to see the opportunities that my grandfather had.

Interestingly, several more of the military accommodation buildings that had been taken over in the main town by the local authority to provide affordable housing (at the same time as my grandfather had bought up some of them), had now reached their expiry date and become available for sale. Like my grandfather, my father bought up some of these buildings, dismantled them and sold them off as sections. Times had changed and the opportunity that my grandfather had seen and taken was no longer the same. Instead of looking for new opportunities, my father spent most of his life trading his time for money, which is not a good strategy if you wish to be rich and have financial and time freedom in your life. He was effectively self-employed rather than having a business.

"Selling your time for money will never make you rich."
– Calum Kirkness

*"Opportunities don't last forever; they need to be taken when
they arise."*
– Calum Kirkness

*"Just because an opportunity worked in the past, doesn't
mean that it will work now or in the future."*
– Calum Kirkness

My grandparents on my mother's side were born and lived on a small island where they had a small croft and shop. It was where my mother was born and brought up. My mother's parents also bought some land and old, redundant military buildings on the small island after the Second World War, which they later sold up to buy a larger business on the nearby main island within the group of islands. I think this was just before I was born. Generally, people would have seen this as a smart move and progress. However, soon after selling their property and land on the small island, the North Sea Oil Industry was about to be born and a large oil company approached the new owner of the land with a view to purchasing it and building an oil terminal. The land that had little value previously had now become extremely valuable due to its strategic location. The new owner received a large eye-watering sum of money for the land, which set them up and made them wealthy for life. It's not something that I ever heard being discussed or seemed to have any effect on the family, but I am sure it must have crossed their minds sometimes. I can only imagine it would be like playing the lottery and winning the jackpot, and then remembering that you have given your lottery ticket away. You win some, you lose some! The lesson that I take from this is that once you own land, never sell it unless you must. Borrow against it to fund your next venture. Family wealth is built up over generations, but of course this also comes with its challenges. I will talk more about money mindset later in the book.

My grandparents went on to build up a successful business in their new shop due to its strategic location on the larger island. It was in a small village, but it was situated on the edge of the main road between the two largest towns. Despite the small village location, it had one of the highest fuel sales on the island. Location is key when you are running a mini-market, fuel and garage business operating a property investment and development business or virtually any type of business for that matter. I also learned that there was never much profit to be made in fuel sales, but it was the fuel that brought a large percentage of the customers to the shop, where they would purchase more goods and services. The shop was also the centre of the community, where the locals would congregate and put the world to rights. My grandfather was a people person, with a laid-back approach to life. He was a very kind, likeable person, whereas my grandmother was very hard-working and could be cruel and unfair at times. She had her favourites and you were ok if she liked you, but you could forget it if she didn't!

My passion for business, money and success was so great that I started working with one of my neighbours on his oyster farm when I was 12 years old. I would come home from school and go straight to work; in my school holidays I would work full-time and sometimes 70 to 80 hours per week. You might be reading this and thinking that is wrong for someone of that age, but no one was forcing me. It was what I wanted to do and there is no question that I sacrificed my teenage years for it. However, by the time I left school, I already had more money than the majority of working families. Depending on the nature of the work we were doing, some of the time I was selling my time for money, and at other times, I was being paid based on results. I was working long hours and some weeks earning more than a working man's wage. I also started my first entrepreneurial joint venture at 13 years old, without understanding what it was at the time. I would take the scrap wood in my father's workshop and make small wooden wheelbarrows, which I then sold in the local craft shop on a 50:50 split on the selling price. I also bought a welding machine and taught myself how to weld and started making and selling small car trailers.

I saved up my money and learned the power of the compound effect from the interest that I was earning from my money in a savings account. Interest rates were high back in the 1980s, and I was happy to see the benefit of my bank balance increasing each month, but I didn't realise or understand it was the compound effect working in my favour back then. When I was 16, I made a big mistake and used a large part of my savings to buy a car to learn to drive in. I wasn't of age, but there were private places to learn. Then, aged 17, I made the same mistake again, but even bigger this time, by purchasing a brand-new car with a loan. I had a passion for cars, which I had also inherited from my father and grandfather. That same amount of money that had been growing and compounding interest was now a depreciating liability, and the compound effect was now working against me. Buying new cars is a regular mistake that I continued to make, however I have finally learned the lesson!

"The earlier in life you learn the power of the compound effect,
the earlier you will achieve financial freedom."
– Calum Kirkness

"The earlier in life you learn about the difference
between assets and liabilities,
the sooner you will reach financial freedom."
– Calum Kirkness

When I was 15, I left school, against my mother's wishes, and joined my father's building company as an apprentice carpenter and joiner. At the time, the UK economy was in recession, and inflation and interest rates were sky high, in double-digit figures – a far cry from today's interest and inflation rates. Margaret Thatcher was Prime Minister and she introduced the Youth Training Scheme (YTS) to help young school leavers into apprenticeships. The government paid the apprentice £25 a week in year one, and 50% of the year was spent at the building college. In year two, the weekly allowance increased to £35, and 25% of the year was spent at building college. Then, in year three, the employer paid the apprentice their weekly wage (which I think was around £48 from memory), and 100% of the year was spent on-site with the employer. This was my opportunity to leave school! I had taken a pay cut to do so as I was now earning less than what I had been earning from ages 12 to 15, but I believed it was good for my future. At the same time, I can remember that Margaret Thatcher's government had an entrepreneur scheme to support those who were unemployed to start up their own business. I think they received £50 per week for one year to help them get off the ground.

My apprenticeship was a tough one and there were many arguments between me and my father, but I learned a lot of valuable skills and lessons during that time. I was fortunate that one of my father's main customers was a successful businessman who was making a lot of money in several different sectors from various ventures and then investing the profits into purchasing large commercial premises in the main town and converting and renovating the buildings to form office, retail and residential units, for short-term and long-term rent. There was a lot of grant funding available at the time for converting and renovating property to create residential and self-catering accommodation. The company we were doing the work for was expert in gaining grant funding and they were building a money-making machine.

Government grant funding is much less available today than it was back in the 1980s and early 1990s. They grabbed the opportunity and reaped the rewards and got the compound effect working massively in their favour.

My grandfather's business model was to buy land, develop properties and sell them. I was now learning the buy, renovate and hold model of property investing. As I shared above, my grandfather's wealth went into decline in retirement, whereas I am fairly sure their passive income stream and wealth would continue to increase in retirement for the family that were using the buy, renovate and hold model, plus they would still have the assets to pass on to the next generation or sell.

I was also fascinated to see how some people were making lots of money in the fishing and oil industry in the 1980s and 1990s. The fishing industry would go into decline in the 1990s: fishermen were struggling as their quotas had been reduced, whilst boats from other countries could come in and wipe out the stock; UK boat owners were being given incentives to scrap their boats. Good boats that had cost hundreds of thousands, and even millions, to build were being taken to scrap yards and destroyed for their scrap value.

When my apprenticeship was complete, I left my father's company and went to work for a different building company for a short period of around nine months before starting my own building and property development company. I had been doing carpentry and joinery work for customers in the evenings and weekends and by the time I left my employment, I had enough work to keep me going for quite a few months, so the risk was much less than a straight jump from employment to self-employment. If you really want something you will find a way, and if you don't, you will come up with excuses. It is rare now to find people who are willing to put in the effort in their spare time to make the transition from employee to self-employed or business owner, smoother and less risky.

Having a job as an employee is something that I have always struggled with: it feels like a prison sentence that robs me of my freedom. I am much happier when I am being an entrepreneur looking for opportunities and solutions to help others. Sometimes the entrepreneur journey can be financially challenging, which means that you need to go back in to periods of employment, but it's important to look on it as a temporary measure and the shorter the better. Don't make the mistake of staying in there any longer than is necessary! The more liabilities and stuff that you buy, the more likely you are to have to go back into employment to get back on track with reaching your goals!

> *"Life is always happening for us, not to us."*
> **– Calum Kirkness**

> *"I would always recommend keeping family*
> *and business separate."*
> **– Calum Kirkness**

> *"Having a regular job will never make you rich*
> *and robs you of your freedom."*
> **– Calum Kirkness**

I was young, ambitious, motivated, driven and hungry for success and over the next few years, I worked crazy hours each week to build up my business. I had endless energy fuelled by ambition and positive stress!

In 1993, the opportunity came for me to purchase a plot of development land. I remember sitting in my lawyer's office, at the opposite side of the desk from him, going through the legal details of the land purchase. Throughout the process, I was thinking back to my grandfather's business model and success, as well as the success of the family that we had developed many properties for during my apprenticeship. I was confident that I was making a good investment decision.

The same plot today would be valued at around five or six times what it was valued at in 1993, and most of the capital growth happened between then and 2008. I am sure you will agree that a 500% return on your investment in 15, or even 25, years is an excellent result and one that the stock market would struggle to match. This is not a one-off land opportunity or stroke of luck, and I share more examples in my Amazon #1 bestselling property investment book, *Property Success Insider Formula*.

Following the purchase of the land and developing the property, I made several big personal and business mistakes, which were expensive and difficult lessons to learn. One was overwork which led to burnout and breakdown. My ambition, hunger and drive for success that had been fuelling my energy to work crazy hours had peaked and was now taking a heavy toll on both my mental and physical health. It was like driving around in a performance car one moment and sitting in one with a blown-up engine the next! I was suffering from deep depression, high levels of anxiety, chronic fatigue and a loss of self-belief and confidence. The business and property development had become a burden and I was no longer able to work. My business became dormant and the property development came to a standstill. Despite feeling burnt out, I was determined to hang on to my business and property and was desperately searching for a way to get my health, self-esteem and confidence back on track. When you have abused your health and effectively blown up your engine, it doesn't matter how much fuel you try adding, you are going nowhere until you have repaired the engine. I will discuss how stress can be both positive and negative and its effects later in this book and how it is never the size of our problems that is the problem; it is only ever the size of us and our ability to be able to handle our problems.

I have seen many entrepreneurs over the years making the same mistakes that I made. We often hear that achieving success is all about working hard, constant hustle and grind 16 hours a day, 7 days a week, etc., and then people are boasting about it on social media to get attention. This is not how success is created. You need to think smart and work smart: 20% of our actions create 80% of our results. This book is all about building a business that you can work on rather than work in and will operate without your presence to give you the time and financial freedom to live life on your own terms. Let your results do the talking.

"Never sacrifice your health in the pursuit of wealth. When you destroy your health to make money, you will lose your income and have to spend the money you made in the process to get your health back and it's not a quick process – work smarter not harder."

– Calum Kirkness

Fast-forward to Friday 1st September 1995 when I was sitting at home on the living room floor. To those looking in from the outside, my life probably looked good, but I was feeling lost, tired, frustrated and desperate for answers and a solution. I was looking through the newspapers and Friday was jobs advertisement day. I thought I needed a new job in a new location to kick-start myself back into action! Jobs for carpenters were plentiful at the time and carpentry was what I knew – it was within my comfort zone. But I also knew deep inside that it was not really the answer. Whilst looking through the newspaper, something else caught my eye. It was an advertisement for last-minute places at Glasgow College of Building and Printing to Study HNC in Building Inspection and Supervision. Now this advert was instantly and directly talking to me!

My best friend, who had been with me through thick and thin over the years was with me, and he was never shy to share his opinion, so I thought I'd better ask for his advice on this idea. I explained that I had seen this advert to study for an HNC in Building Inspection and Supervision. He immediately replied "WHAT? You going to college? You're not clever enough; you left school at 15. And what about your business and property? You'll end up losing everything and what will people think?!"

I sat in silence for a moment, thinking, 'These are valid points, BUT...'

And then I replied, "I have always listened to your advice in the past and look where it has got me! I am a complete wreck in every way!"

So I told my ego where to go on this occasion. I faced my fears and grabbed this opportunity. It turned out to be a good one. Our intuition is always guiding us and when we are on the right track we will feel at ease and when we are off track this is when we feel dis-ease.

"Be careful when listening to your ego, it is there to protect
you, not to help you create success."
– Calum Kirkness

I called the college and was invited for an interview in person the following Tuesday. I went for the interview and was accepted. Success! The course was due to start the following Monday, 8th September 1996. I had just a few days to get back home, prepare my things, arrange accommodation and travel back to Glasgow. I managed to gather the strength and motivation to pull it all together.

"Never underestimate your own strength. You are much
stronger than you think."
– Calum Kirkness

"Our environment where we live and spend a lot of time has a
big impact on the rest of our life and our success or failure."
– Calum Kirkness

College was the perfect opportunity for me at the time, and I am very grateful that I grabbed it. It got me out of my normal environment, and it required me to use my brain whilst resting my body. I performed well and graduated with merit, which was the highest pass mark possible. It was a much-needed boost to my knowledge and confidence.

I was now making progress in the recovery of my health, but was still not fully fit and healthy, so I thought I would like to use my qualifications to get me entry to University. I applied to study BSc in Quantity Surveying at Abertay University in Dundee and was accepted straight into year two due to my qualifications and industry experience. I settled in quickly and was performing well.

"Believe in yourself and never underestimate your abilities."
– Calum Kirkness

At the end of my first year at university, I got the opportunity to take a gap year and work as a Clerk of Works in the Major Works Building Department at the Orkney Islands Council (OIC). The Council was undertaking its largest capital works expenditure programme to date, and I was fortunate to be involved in several large and smaller new-build commercial buildings. It was a great opportunity and learning experience for me and gave me insights into how local government worked. I share more about different management and operational structures later in the book.

During my time in the temporary Clerk of Works position, a full-time C.O.W position came up and I was encouraged to apply for it. It seemed a great opportunity to have a safe, secure job and have a regular income with pension benefits. From the way we are brought up and educated, It made complete logical sense, so I applied for the job and got it. It soon became apparent that something wasn't right for me, and my health started to deteriorate again. I was left facing another tough decision: whether to go back to university and complete my degree in Quantity Surveying or accept where I was. I knew deep inside that going back to university would be the right decision even if it didn't seem the right logical answer! I am very grateful that I made the choice to go back to university to complete my degree. If I hadn't taken this opportunity at the time, I am sure I would have always looked back with regret. Our minds never like unfinished business. One year later, I graduated with the BSc in Quantity Surveying, with Distinction, which was the highest pass grade possible.

University Graduation – BSc in Quantity Surveying with Distinction

During my time at university and working for the OIC, I had managed to make progress and finish the house I was building. During this period, a local farmer who was retiring from his nearby farm, had approached me several times to see if I would sell the house. He could see his farm from the house that I was building, and it had fantastic views. The first few times I was reluctant to sell, despite the property feeling like it was a heavy burden. I had made the mistake of investing too much of my own time, labour and emotion into building it and my personal life was in a mess and very challenging at the time. I carried out most of the works myself to save money, which meant that I had built the property at a low cost and on paper made a nice profit. I paid a high price though in terms of my health and lost several years' income, which was much more than the profit that I made from the house. I later agreed to sell the house to the farmer.

Looking back, I learned that there are different levels of motivation. Just because someone is not motivated to sell today, doesn't mean they won't become motivated later. This is valuable to understand when dealing with motivated sellers in both property and business and when selling new products and services to customers.

My first project as a property developer. The house I sold to the retiring farmer.

"Leave emotion out of investing decisions."

"One of the biggest things that holds us back is forming attachment to things."
– Calum Kirkness

"Let go of anything that is weighing you down and move on."
– Calum Kirkness

"One of the hardest things to do sometimes is letting go, but it can also be the thing that sets you free."
– Calum Kirkness

"There are different levels of motivation. A 'no' today does not mean a 'no' tomorrow, next week or next month."
– Calum Kirkness

"Always follow up on leads even after an initial 'no' response."
– Calum Kirkness

Following the sale of my land and house, I thought to myself: 'There must be easier ways of making money than running a construction company and developing property!' I used the profits made from the house sale to invest in several other different asset classes. They were a mixture of low, medium and high-risk investments that all turned out to be a complete or significant disaster.

"Only invest in things that you understand yourself with people that you know and can demonstrate results."

– Calum Kirkness

Most people today are passive investors handing over their money each month to a pension fund that they do not understand anything about, which is being run by a person when they do not even know their name, past history or results.

After losing most of my money, I decided to cash in what was left, or what I could still access, and thought maybe property was not as bad after all! Over the next few years, I started to buy some development land again and took some big risks. The first site that I bought was a brownfield commercial site in the main town. The site was in a good, residential area with no other commercial buildings nearby. My plans for the site were to either turn the existing buildings into apartments or knock down the buildings and build new residential apartments. I have since been offered eight times the value of what I paid for the site. A few years ago, I applied for planning permission to build eight apartments on the site, which was refused planning permission by the planning committee despite the application being recommended for approval by the planning officers. Planning can be a political process.

Shortly after buying the development site mentioned above, I purchased another brownfield commercial site on the edge of a village. I could see the potential of this site, but it wasn't mortgageable as there was a block on development in the village until the mains sewer had been upgraded, which was thought to be a few years away, but turned out to be six years. It was a good location and I was determined to buy the site, so I bought it using three separate personal loans and paid significantly more than the market value at the time to secure the purchase.

Once the main sewer had been upgraded, I secured planning consent for nine large, luxury apartments and a conference centre on the site and made the mains sewer connection. This all happened shortly before the peak of the market in 2008. I had cleared the site and had everything in place to start, except for the structural engineer's certificate, which was delaying the final issue of the Building Warrant Approval to allow the works to start. Thankfully, I had a written, detailed and signed contract in place with them, which I had negotiated well. I also plan to go ahead with this multi-million-pound development project soon.

"In my experience, property investment is the best and safest investment."
– Calum Kirkness

"Buy property based on location, location, location."
– Calum Kirkness

"There is no such thing as get rich quick."
– Calum Kirkness

"Business and the planning process can be a political process."
– Calum Kirkness

"Get all contracts in writing."
– Calum Kirkness

"The greatest risk to your future is taking no risk. When we take no risk and allow fear to dictate our future, we end up risking everything."
– Calum Kirkness

In 2005, I purchased another building company, taking over their employees, workshop, tools and equipment and contracts. I didn't buy it as a going concern to ensure that there would be no responsibility or liability for past contracts. The economy was booming and it was a great way to increase the workforce at a time when it was difficult to find additional employees. I had also seen value in having access to lease the workshop, which I needed at the time. I paid a sum for the value of getting the lease on the workshop and some for the value in the new contracts, but nothing for the goodwill as I viewed that as being tied to and going with the previous owner. I share more on selling a business in a later chapter in this book. Over the course of the next six months, I amalgamated the new company into my existing company. Bringing two companies together is not an easy process as the two workforces will have different ways of working, different terms and conditions, and feel resistant to change. Most people tend to feel uncomfortable and unsettled with change happening. With hindsight, I should have sold the combined business in 2007 when it and the economy was at its peak.

Over the next few years, I continued to invest in buying development land, off-plan property and newly-completed properties, which have all been very good investment decisions. Some property investors will advise you to avoid these options. There are things you need to understand about the market before investing, but when you time the market well, they can work well and in your favour.

Since the year 2000 to date, I have worked on many multi-million-pound property development projects, which has allowed me to gain an in-depth knowledge of the residential and commercial property sectors as well as various other commercial business sectors such as leisure, health and fitness, retail, private hospitals, etc.

In 2014, I decided to take a step back and look at the larger picture. I could see that things were changing, and we were in a new era of the information age and thought it was time to take a look at where the opportunities were and adapt. Over the last few years, I have invested a lot of my time and money into my own personal development, hiring business coaches and mentors, and learning how to develop my business and property knowledge into training products and services.

A few years back, I was looking at how Warren Buffett operated and how he had become the richest man in the world in 2008, but now sits at number 3 having been overtaken by Jeff Bezos of Amazon and Bill Gates of Microsoft (according to Wikipedia and Forbes). Warren Buffett spends most of his time reading, researching and investing in businesses. He considers the best investment that you can ever make is in yourself and considers public speaking to be one of the most valuable skills to have. I took notice of what he was saying, invested in my personal development and got myself trained as a world-class public speaker.

If you want to become successful, a good tip is to listen to what those who are already successful are saying and doing, then model their success around your passions and natural strengths and talents. Warren Buffet was Bill Gates's mentor and now he is richer than Warren Buffett. They are great friends.

The fastest route to achieving success is to get a mentor who is genuinely interested in you and views your success as their success, and who is not afraid that you will become more successful than them. These types of mentors and coaches are hard to find, but they do exist. In life, you either pay in time or money and it's important to remember that time is our most valuable asset. Once it is gone it's gone. But when you invest time and money in your personal development, it can come back in multiples and free up a lot of your time in the future.

I was interested in learning the value of intellectual property and the technology of how I could productise my knowledge and reach lots of people with it in order to help them. Most people are sitting on a wealth of knowledge and experience, which has significant value, without them realising or fully appreciating this. There are people out there who can benefit from your knowledge, experience and story. The power of technology can allow you to release the value of your knowledge and experience by creating electronic products that can reach and help millions of people. It has never been easier to build a business and reach millions of people. Your shop front can be a webpage or website, you can use a YouTube account as your own TV channel, your podcast as your radio station, and then there is Facebook, Instagram and LinkedIn, etc., to help you build your brand and carry out targeted marketing that would have costs tens of thousands previously. Even publishing a book is now possible and available to virtually everyone thanks to Amazon and the like. We are living in incredible times, where you don't even need to be a tech expert any more to set it all up and reap the rewards of sharing your knowledge and expertise with lots of people.

Today, I continue to invest in business and property and I am now also building up my new business around the information and technology sectors to develop products and services to share my knowledge and experience with others. This will help them succeed in business and property investment and create the time and financial freedom to live life on their own terms. I hope that you will be one of them and that I will have the pleasure of meeting you at one of my live events soon.

"The best investment that you can ever make is in yourself, the second-best investment that you can make is in property, and the best way to make the money to invest is having your own business."
– Calum Kirkness

"Having great communication and negotiation skills is key to succeed in business."
– Calum Kirkness

"Model the success of people who have already reached the level that you would like to reach and got there by a means that you would be happy to model and follow."
– Calum Kirkness

My Top 25 Mistakes

Here are the top 25 mistakes that I have made and learned the biggest lessons from along the way. They are in no particular order:

1. Selling my time for money.
2. Overwork and burn-out.
3. Not trusting my intuition more.
4. Staying in or going back to periods of employment for too long.
5. Not following my passions.
6. Not focusing on using my natural strengths and talents to maximum effect.
7. Not outsourcing more earlier.
8. Staying In my comfort zone.

9.   Giving up on some things too early.

10. Not learning the skill and art of public speaking earlier.

11. Not specialising and focusing on niche markets earlier.

12. Not developing products earlier.

13. Being too afraid to stand out.

14. Worrying about what other people would think or say.

15. Not engaging in personal development earlier.

16. Not having coaches and mentors earlier.

17. Spending too much money on buying new cars.

18. Not mastering delegation earlier.

19. Not mastering management earlier.

20. Not developing systems earlier.

21. Not setting healthy boundaries. (Saying "No" more).

22. Not building and maintaining better relationships.

23. Not writing books and becoming an author earlier.

24. Not always believing in myself.

25. Thinking that life needed to be logical and not having the faith to believe that life is magical.

It is human to make mistakes and I am sure I will make some more. The key is to always be learning and growing and making more good choices than mistakes.

Success in life comes from making just a few great business and investment decisions and making less bad choices and decisions in other areas.

This chapter alone contains many valuable business, investment and life lessons that you can use to create a successful life for yourself.

CHAPTER 2

SOLUTION

All business, at its most basic level, comes down to providing a solution in the form of a product or service that solves a problem or meets the needs of a customer at the right time.

Unless you can SOLVE A PROBLEM or MEET A CUSTOMER'S NEED in a cost-effective and efficient manner that there is enough demand for and provides your customers with more value than the price they pay, you do not have a sustainable business. Price is what we pay, value is what we receive.

> *"The bigger the problem that you can solve for the most amount of people, the bigger the reward."*
> **– Calum Kirkness**

> *"If you want to be rich, you need to create a solution to a problem that becomes a money-making machine."*
> **– Calum Kirkness**

Most business owners find themselves stuck in their business rather than being able to work on it due to not fully understanding how to productise, systemise and automate the solutions that they are offering to their customers. This places restrictions and limits on the rate and growth level that a business can achieve.

Many self-employed and small business owners are surviving rather than thriving due to offering products and services which require their time in exchange for money, or too much of their own input in running the business. To have a business that frees up your time, it is essential that it is productised, systemised and automated in some areas, which is covered in greater detail later throughout this book.

To have a real business, it is essential that you provide a product and/or service that is based on the value that the customer receives and is not based on selling your time for money.

Before anything else, coming up with the right idea at the right time is key to the outcome and creating a scalable business, which is why this is the first step in the process and the rest will follow.

I come across many people who would like to be an entrepreneur, or who are already an entrepreneur, and they generally fall in to one of four categories:

1. Those who want to have a business but don't have an idea or the knowledge.
2. Those who have an idea but don't have the business knowledge.
3. Those who have business knowledge but don't have an idea.
4. Those who are a combination of the above but don't have the right mindset, which means they are being held back by their fears and limiting beliefs.

The perfect ingredients and recipe for making a successful business include:

- Idea
- Knowledge
- Mindset
- Passion and Desire
- Natural Strengths
- Time

A person who wants to be an entrepreneur, but fails to act on it, is just a wantrepreneur.

The key to being a successful entrepreneur is finding OPPORTUNITY WHERE OTHERS FAIL TO NOTICE OR FAIL TO ACT. The solution should be creative and novel, but must be easily understood by potential customers.

There is no lack of opportunities for those who care to look, listen and learn. Ideas and opportunities can come in all shapes and sizes, from anywhere and at any time. As a business entrepreneur, you are likely to have a unique way of thinking, where your mind rarely switches of from identifying problems and having ideas for creating solutions.

I find that my mind is most creative when I am sitting in silence or out in the countryside where it is quiet and there are few distractions. Most people are now too uncomfortable sitting with just their own company, and end up constantly distracting themselves with social media, television, gossiping about others and anything else where they can shut out or forget about their own thoughts.

There is no greater destroyer of our genius, creativity and intuition than being a busy fool, distracting ourselves with nonsense, and then complaining that the world is a difficult and unfair place to live in because it is not presenting us with the same opportunities as others. The truth is that everyone is being presented with opportunities, but not everyone is able to see them and not everyone has the courage to act on them.

We are natural-born creative geniuses with potential beyond our wildest imaginations. Our soul intuition is always guiding us, but it doesn't shout like the ego – it whispers – so we also need to be in silence or in a positive, inspirational environment to feel and understand the message.

If you are still searching for the seed from which to start up and grow your business, I have developed a process to help you identify problems and come up with solutions, which I have set out below:

Step 1 – Problem

A good place to start identifying problems is by considering the sector of the market where you have gained the most knowledge, experience and contacts. Secondly, look to the most promising sectors of the market and identify what problem areas still exist in each of them. Some of the top market sectors going forward, in no particular order, are likely to be:

- Technology
- Media
- Health
- Fitness
- Leisure
- Fashion
- Relationships

- Property
- Construction
- Energy
- Travel
- Transportation
- Finance
- Retail (Online)
- Personal Development

Ways to identify opportunities to come up with solutions to solve problems or fill needs could be:

1. Identify a problem that you have experienced yourself. Maybe you cannot find a product or service that solves your problem or fills your needs.
2. Listen to what other people are talking and complaining about the most.
3. Ask people what their biggest problems and challenges are.

As a business entrepreneur, instead of viewing problems as problems, start viewing all problems as potential opportunities.

Once you have identified a problem, there are several key items that need to be established.

- Is there already a product or service exists that you can offer to meet the needs of the customer on trade-to-customer or commission basis. A good example of this would be a car franchise that is not offered yet in a town or city that is large enough to sustain it. In this example, the car manufacturer provides the product and marketing content and material, and you would provide the sales and service.
- Is there a product or service that already exists but is not ideal and could be improved upon?
- If there is no product or service that exists to solve the problem or fill the need? Do you have the necessary skills, knowledge, experience to create the solution and deliver it in the form of a product or service?

- Do you feel passionate about providing the solution and is it something that you will enjoy doing?
- Are you willing to learn the knowledge required and gain any missing skills?
- Determine the size of the potential market for your products and/or services and assess if it is large enough to be profitable, sustainable and meet your goals.
- Is the issue a problem for a business or customer?
- Would the business be Business to Customer (B2C) or Business to Business (B2B)

Brainstorming with other like-minded entrepreneurs or working with a coach or mentor can be very useful in helping to identify problems. Come up with ideas to solve them that can be monetised to create and build a successful business. I strongly recommend having the support of a coach or mentor and attending mastermind group sessions with other like-minded entrepreneurs. I will go into more details on support and networking later in the book.

Once you have identified where you can potentially solve a problem or fill a need in the market, the diagram below is a useful tool to help you identify your sweet spot, where you can serve the needs of others and by turning your passions and natural strengths and talents into profit.

Step 2 – Pain

Once you have identified the problem, the next step is to determine the level of pain that people have from it and the impact that it has on their lives. The pain could be mild, moderate, significant or even severe.

The bigger the pain that can be solved, the bigger the reward.

Step 3 – Perspective / Projection

The next step is to put the problem and the pain into perspective to assess the level of opportunity that it could provide. This involves looking at the following:

- Minor pain, minor demand – unlikely to be viable.
- Minor pain, significant demand – may be viable, worth looking at.
- Severe pain, low demand – may be viable, worth looking at.
- Severe pain, significant demand – almost certainly viable and worth looking at.

Step 4 – Product

The next step (once the opportunity has been assessed as being a good potential opportunity) is to develop the product and service that solves the problem or meets the need.

Solutions to problems can be offered at three different levels:

1. Do it yourself – This is where you provide the customer with the solution in the form of knowledge or goods, which they then implement themselves. To give you some examples:

- This book could be considered a DIY solution as I am offering you the business information and knowledge, but it is up to you to apply the knowledge yourself to start and build your business.
- A recipe for a cake would be another DIY product.

Do-it-yourself products are great for cash-poor time-rich customers.

2. Do it with you – This is where you provide the customer with the solution and help them implement it. For example:

- A coaching programme to help you implement the information in this book and provide you with support to establish your business would be a do-it-with-you product.
- Another example would be to offer the ingredients for the cake premixed, ready to bake.

Do it with you products are great for average-income customers who have some time available.

3. Do it for you – This is where the customer understands what he wants, but does not have the time or desire to implement it and you provide the full service to them. For example:

- This would be where I would do everything required to help you develop your product or service, set up the company for you and provide the support to keep the business running smoothly.
- Another example would be to sell a cake ready-made for the customer to eat.

Do-it-for-you products and services are good for cash-rich time-poor customers.

The diagram below provides an illustration of where DIY, DWY and DFY products and services fit each customer profile best in terms of time and income.

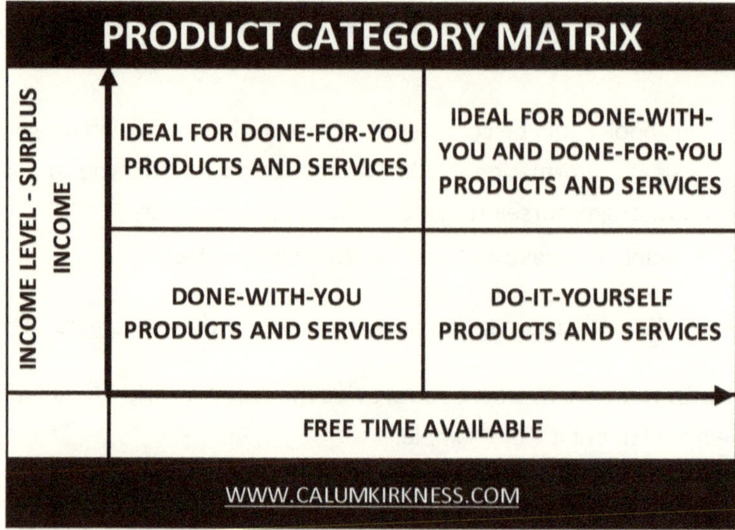

Step 5 – Customer-Pleasure-Received Matrix

Business opportunities also exist for providing pleasurable experiences for customers to fill a need. It is important to consider the level of pleasure that the customer would receive and the level of demand to assess the viability of the opportunity. The diagram below illustrates the relationship between pleasure and demand and likely viability of the opportunity.

Step 6 – Passion

Do you feel passionate about developing the product and offering the service? If you do, go ahead and test your ideas. If you don't feel passionate about them but do feel that the idea has great potential, you could possibly look at developing the solution with a view to rapidly building up the business and selling it quickly. You could also look to do a joint venture with another organisation or investor who is passionate about the area of business. This strategy needs careful consideration as it could lumber you with a burden that you are not passionate about, which will weigh you down and prevent you from taking other opportunities that are more suited towards your genius.

Once you have identified a single or multiple problems and/or needs and potential solutions, and you feel passionate about delivering them, it is helpful to make a full list of ideas to rank and assess on what is going to be best for the market, the customer and you.

The next step is testing your ideas. Even the best business ideas, products and services need to be tested before they are fully implemented, in order to reduce risk.

I come across some enthusiastic entrepreneurs who think they have come up with the most amazing idea that they need to keep secret until they are ready to launch it to the market and take the world by storm. They eventually find out that there is either no market or not a sustainable market there to make the venture viable and they end up losing a lot of time, money and effort in the process. It is important to remember that business is about what the market and customer thinks is a great solution, and not your own idea of what the customer should think is a great solution.

The reality is, there is no way of knowing for sure that a business idea will succeed unless you test it first. It's crucial to confirm that there is a space and demand for your projected product or service in the market – and whether your intended customers care at all about whatever you want to sell to them.

A good business opportunity is one that:

- Has many potential customers with real needs.
- Has customers who you can easily identify and find.
- Has customers who have money to buy your products or services.
- Allows you to make and sell your product at a profit.
- Can result in enough sales to enough customers fast enough.
- Allows you to earn your required income level.
- Is something you are qualified to do.
- Is something that you are passionate about delivering.
- Has little competition or competition that is providing a beatable service.

CHAPTER 3

SURVEY

Surveying yourself, your idea, your key strengths and weaknesses, your potential market, and your potential customers are all equally important. You may have key strengths but no potential customers, or lots of potential customers but not the right strengths. The key is finding a market with lots of potential customers that you are passionate about and can serve with your natural strengths and talents.

There are multiple ways to learn about and obtain information on the potential demand for your product or service. Here are the steps to take to test your business idea before you invest time, money, and resources into it.

Identify your ideal customer, which includes identifying:

- Location
- Age
- Gender
- Relationship / Marital Status
- Employment status
- Income bracket
- Interests
- Where they hang out
- Where they currently obtain similar products

All the above are key to the outcome of the results. For example: if your product is designer wedding dresses, you wouldn't survey retired men to test the demand. You would be better surveying single women between 20 and 40 in high-income areas who are interested in getting married.

Who will your competitors be?

Are you a quality or quantity person, i.e low volume, high quality? Or high volume, low quality? For example: Renault would be high volume low quality when compared to Rolls Royce, which would be low volume high quality. You can see that both companies build cars, but they have very different target markets. Renault customers will have a different set of data to Rolls Royce and the marketing requirements to reach their customers are different.

Identifying your potential competitors early on will not only help you identify how to measure your testing—it will help you narrow down your customer base as well. Competitor metrics can serve as a baseline to compare your test results. The customers of your potential competitors will most likely be the customers you'll want. Finding future customers to test your business idea on could be as easy as finding your future competitors' customers.

Here are a few ways to analyse the competition:

- What do they do well?
- Where are they failing?
- Can you compete with them?
- Can you use your findings to your advantage?

Depending on the size of the market, if it is large enough, you can look to identify a sector and niche it down until you have identified a specific section and customer set that you would like to do business with.

> *"80% of your turnover and profits will come from 20% of your customers. Focus on finding and identifying the 20% that you wish to attract and serve."*
> **– Calum Kirkness**

You don't need to have everything in place or be able to see the outcome. This is where faith and belief play a large part. You also don't need to be great to start. If you have the vision and belief and approach each stage with passion, positivity, persistence and commitment, the road ahead will unfold before you and you will become greater and wiser along the journey. When you later look back, you will see how the dots magically connected, that could never have been logically planned out at the start of the journey. For example, there is a big difference between the first iPhone or Samsung Galaxy and the current versions. But the current versions wouldn't exist had the first versions not been launched when they were.

This highlights another important point that competition is not necessarily a bad thing. It can be used to push the boundaries to be consistently improving by redesign and tweaking your product(s) and services to be continuously irresistible to your customers … which means you must get to know your customers in a new way. You must create what is called a Customer Avatar, or a persona of your ideal customer – then build your product or service specifically for them. You must also go on to understand what I call your Customer Influencer, or the person who influences your customer most, so you can really get into the psychology of why your customer is buying.

Finally, you must release that all-important NEXT product, and build what I call the graduation model in your business. To succeed, you must have a product path that your customers can take to get more and better results. We will look at these areas in more detail in later chapters of the book.

How do you know if you have a good idea for a business? – The best way is to test it.

It is the customers who know best what they need. Your job is to provide them with what they need.

Most entrepreneurs in the world never lack having new ideas. It is the figuring out and deciding which ideas are worth spending time and money on to take forward that is the difficult part.

It is the same scenario whether you are a cash-strapped start-up that's funded with credit cards and loans from banks, friends and family, or the next blockbuster out of Silicon Valley that's sitting on a war-chest of millions in venture capital funding.

No matter who you are or how big you hope to grow your business, figuring out what product to build and what services to offer is a big challenge.

You could just rely on your gut feeling – and sometimes that's not a bad option and I do encourage that – but it is also good to back it up with some logic gained from surveying your potential market. Since most businesses fail within five years of starting, it is well worth taking a few extra steps to discover if you really have a great idea before you risk your time and money.

Here's my guide to figuring out if your idea is any good and if it's worth moving to the next level.

Business Idea Validation

Step 1 - Start by documenting your key assumptions about your business, products and services.

When you are first considering a new business idea and looking at the products and services that you could potentially offer, there is little value in spending time preparing a formal business plan until you have surveyed and tested the market with your idea. A good place to start is with a Lean Plan and a simple elevator pitch to jot down the basic components of your idea. As a minimum, you'll want to cover the following:

- **Why are you doing this?** What's your mission? All new businesses need a sense of purpose. Are you trying to improve people's lives in some way? What are the core differentiators of your business that set you apart from the next person trying to build a similar business?

- **What problem are you solving?** You need to be solving some sort of real problem that exists in the world. If you aren't solving a problem for potential customers, then how will you get people to buy your product or service?

- **Who are you solving this problem for?** As important as having a problem to solve, is having enough customers that have this problem. Knowing who your ideal customer is and how you can find them is critical to starting a successful business.

- **How are your potential customers solving their problem today?** This is where you want to write down a few notes about your competition. What choices do your customers have today? How is your solution better?

- **Do you think you can make money?** You don't need to worry at this early stage about in-depth financial forecasts, but you should carry out some basic calculations to make sure your idea can be profitable.

- The key to this initial step is to write down your key assumptions quickly—You don't need a lot of time or need to write a lot (certainly not more than a page). Just get your ideas out there so that you are clear about your key assumptions because the next steps involve getting out into the real world and seeing if your beliefs are accurate.

Step 2 - Talk to your potential customers.

Surprisingly, talking to potential customers about your new business idea is the step that many entrepreneurs skip in order to protect their idea. Not talking to your potential customers to test your idea significantly increases your chances of failure, so after you have validated your ideas, the sooner you head out of the door and start talking to people the better.

When you speak with your potential customers, you're trying to validate the key assumptions that you made when coming up with the solutions to the problems that you have identified. It is important to find out if they do have the problem you assumed that they have. How do they currently solve their problem today? And what do they think of your idea?

By talking to as many potential customers as you can, you get multiple points of view, which is valuable information to have.

As you learn about your potential customers, you should be continuously reviewing and updating your definition of the customer problem, your solution, the competition and your pitch.

Step 3 - Show your prospective customers a prototype of your product, if you have one.

If you can, share an example of your solution in the form of a product or service. This is beneficial in getting potential customers on the same page as you and to better critique your idea and solution. If you're building a product, maybe you can share a prototype or some images of what the product looks like.

If you're offering a service, describe what the results of your service are and what the deliverables would be if your prospect hired you.

The more real you can make your idea for your potential customers, the higher the quality of the feedback that you will get.

Step 4 - Figure out what people would be willing to pay.

As you talk to your potential customers, try and figure out what they might be willing to pay for your solution. This can be tricky, because ideally everyone wants everything for free! But there are some strategies to obtain the information without asking the question outright. First, if there are competitors in your market, you can look at their pricing and then decide how you want to differentiate your company. You can also look at the value you are providing to your customer and create a price based on that.

When you have a price in mind for your product and services, you can ask your prospective customer if they would order your product or service right now for your price. You might find that people will say, "yes" right away, or they will tell you what they think the price should be. By paying close attention to their response, you will be able to assess if the customer thinks they are getting a good deal or if your price is a bit high.

Step 5 - Find people who don't believe in your idea.

This is where finding a few naysayers is important for getting a balanced view. Finding people who don't like your idea and getting them to poke holes in it and share why they don't think it will work, can act as inspiration on how you can improve your idea, products and services.

You don't necessarily have to address all the weak points that detractors point out, but it's important that you gather feedback from people who think you can improve. Not everyone is going to be your customer, but it's better to head into a new business endeavour with your eyes wide open.

Step 6 - Find out how much money is needed to launch your business.

As you gather customer feedback and refine your pitch, you will hopefully be homing in on a great business idea. By vetting and refining your idea before you start your business you are greatly enhancing your chances of success.

By this stage, you should know if you have a winning idea on your hands or not. Now you need to figure out if the business can be financially viable and what funds you need to get it off the ground.

This is the stage where you will need to move beyond your initial business pitch and start building out some detailed financial projections to figure out how much money you'll need to get up and running. As a minimum, you'll want to create a sales forecast, an expense budget, and a cash-flow forecast. These three forecasts will help you figure out what it's going to take to start your business and keep it going as you get your first customers.

Step 7 - Start as small as possible.

It can be tempting to dive in at the deep end and build your complete business the way you imagine it will be. It is advisable to resist this urge if possible and start small and continue to gather feedback from customers, which is a key component to growth. With a smaller start, you'll be able to change direction faster and react to customer feedback quicker and ultimately build a much stronger foundation from which to scale from.

Starting small also gets your solution out into the market quicker. The faster you can get to market, the faster you'll gather feedback.

When you open for business with a "start small" approach, you might feel like you're not "ready." But, often, you'll find that customers won't even notice. Your ability to pivot and change directions quickly is much more valuable to your long-term success than trying to get everything right the first time.

Step 8 - Stay flexible.

The final key to making sure you have a good idea that will grow into a successful business is to stay flexible. The best business owners can keep their ego in check and listen to customer feedback. This doesn't mean that the customer is always right. By listening and being flexible, this will enable you to adapt and change directions as needed. You don't want to react to one customer's opinion, but you do want to look for broader trends in the opinions of as many customers as possible.

You may even decide that certain types of customers aren't part of your target market. For example, you might decide that you only want to sell to bigger businesses, and you can adjust your pricing and marketing to reflect that.

It also means that you don't sit behind your desk building a business plan without getting out and talking to your customers.

Lean Planning at its core is all about starting with just the fundamentals of a plan and then verifying that your idea is good before moving on to the next step.

CHAPTER 4

SWOT ANALYSIS STRENGTHS AND SKILLS

We all have genius within us – our natural strengths, skills and talents – which make it difficult for others to compete with us. We should always be focusing on using our natural strengths, skills and talents and using these to our benefit in both our personal and business life.

It is a sad fact that many people today are more interested in shaping and strengthening their body than they are in improving and shaping their mindset. Whilst I think having a healthy body is important, having a healthy mind and building your character and emotional intelligence is much more important when it comes to achieving success, happiness and fulfilment in business and life in general.

When we spend time focusing on things we do not enjoy, or enjoy but do not do particularly well, we end up procrastinating and going in to a downwards spiral. This is the worst thing we can do for our customers, our success and our happiness. Our weaknesses and the things that we do not enjoy doing should be outsourced to those who can do them much better than us. If you think you cannot afford to outsource the things that you do not enjoy, you will soon end up discovering the high cost of doing them yourself.

"Do what you do best and delegate the rest."
– Calum Kirkness

In the early days, most entrepreneurs, (depending on their level of financial resources) will have to cover most areas of the business themselves, then as the business grows, they can increase the level of areas of the business that they can employ people with the skills to do or outsource them to specialist service providers.

When starting out, you are likely to already have some of the essential skills; others you may know a little and wish to learn and develop, which can be a steep learning curve. Others may be beyond your capabilities or interest, in which case you will need to outsource them or hire employees to do them. Either way, by learning as many of the essential skills as possible, it will help you to understand them at a basic level, which in turn will help you understand what to look for in the process of outsourcing them or hiring employees to do them for you. You will then be in a position to assess if they are performing the task to a satisfactory level.

A good place to start in assessing your strengths and weaknesses is by doing a SWOT analysis. SWOT is an acronym for Strengths, Weaknesses, Opportunities, Threats. It is a relatively straightforward and easy exercise to do. Before we look at SWOT analysis in a bit more detail, let's look at what the essential business skills required are, so that you know what the key items are to include in your analysis:

Essential Business Strengths and Skills Required To Start, Build and Operate a Successful Business:

1. Self-Discipline

Discipline is an important factor in life and only you can discipline yourself. This one cannot be outsourced but having a good personal assistant (PA) and team in place and a good supply chain around you can be a big help. Being an entrepreneur requires you to have discipline for both the small and larger things that you commit to, which is also a great leadership quality to have that sets the standard for others to follow. It all begins with you.

2. Communication and Negotiation

You will be required to have good communication and negotiation skills for dealing with potential investors, consultants, suppliers, customers and employees. Having both effective written and verbal communication skills will help you build good long-term working relationships, which are negotiated on win-win outcomes. Every communication that you have should reflect both the business and personal image, values and branding that you wish to project. All communication and negotiations should be carried out professionally. People will forget what you said, but they will never forget how you made them feel.

3. Project Management and Planning

Starting your own business means that you will have to manage a wide range of projects and be able to prioritise tasks, such as getting the business registered, creating the branding, developing your products and services, setting up websites, developing policies and procedures, etc. Understanding how to effectively manage your resources, including time, money, staff, etc., will help you achieve your goals. The Eisenhower Matrix is a useful tool in helping to prioritise tasks and manage your time.

EISENHOWER MATRIX		
	URGENT	**NON URGENT**
IMPORTANT	**DO IT** today	**SCHEDULE IT** in your diary
NON IMPORTANT	**DELEGATE IT** to someone	**ELIMINATE IT** stop doing it
WWW.CALUMKIRKNESS.COM		

4. Financial Management

Being able to effectively manage the finances of the company is critical to its survival. Initially you will need to be able to calculate the start-up costs and then be able to price your products and/or services, forecast the sales, ongoing costs (both variable and fixed) and the cashflow, as well as monitor profit and loss. Having sound financial management skills will help you operate the business profitably and protect your investment by identifying any weaknesses or problem areas early on, whilst you still have time to take action and make some adjustments to steer things back on course before it is too late. There are some great accountancy software packages and apps that can help you managing your business finances.

5. Sales and Marketing

It is important to have a good sales and marketing plan and strategy in place to promote your products and services effectively to the right audience and then have a good process in place to follow up and secure the sales. This can be challenging, with a steep learning curve for some entrepreneurs. Many people believe that they do not like sales or that they are not good at it. We are all selling ourselves every day. When we find the right product, which we are passionate about, the marketing and sales process becomes much easier. It is all about developing the value for the customer and having the confidence that your products provide so much value that they will become fans. This is contribution as well as serving, which are both satisfying and fulfilling for our human need for growth and contribution. Sales and marketing are covered in more detail later in the book.

6. Customer Service

Great customer service is a valuable skill and every person involved in your business should have it regardless of their position or level within the organisation. Every contact point that you have with the public and your customers is an opportunity to create a positive lasting impact or leave a damaging image or impact. The bigger your business grows, the less direct contact you will have with your customers. However, you should always check in with them yourself from time to time regardless of the size of your business. Jeff Bezos of Amazon is a master of this, and the company is a good example of how to build great customer service. I see many businesses that fail miserably in delivering good customer service to existing customers, whilst spending heavily on marketing to attract new ones. Focusing on your existing customers and turning them into lifelong loyal fans is one of the most important and valuable things that you can do for your business growth and sustainability. Here is a list of some of the top customer service qualities:

- Patience
- A calming presence
- Empathy
- Listening skills
- Ability to understand the customer

- Clear communication skills
- Positive attitude
- Positive language
- Authenticity
- Assertiveness
- Confidence
- Ability to respond quickly
- Ability to act
- Product knowledge
- Problem-solving skills
- Tenacity
- Persuasion
- Willingness to learn from feedback
- Willingness to go the extra mile
- Personal responsibility
- Adaptability
- Desire to learn
- Professionalism
- Time management skills
- The ability to let it go

7. Leadership

When we wish to build a successful business, leadership is another very important quality to have. There are some people who appear to be natural born leaders; however, this is a skill that can be learned and developed with the support of the right coaches and mentors.

Being a business owner means that it is essential that we can lead, motivate and inspire. Great leaders create more leaders, which means that as your business grows you lead from the front, and have the leaders that you have created then coach and mentor the new employees on the company values, systems, goals and vision. This allows the company to grow, but it is important to keep as flat a structure as possible and have an open-door policy, where people can still access you personally regardless of their position in the company or supply chain.

8. Delegation

Failing to delegate is a trap that many new and existing business owners fall into, which is usually due to their reluctance to let go of control as they worry that others won't be able to perform the tasks up to the standards that they would like. Being unable to delegate tasks and responsibilities places huge restrictions on the ability of a business to grow and keeps the owner trapped working in the business rather than working on it. The inability to delegate robs the business owner of the freedom that most entrepreneurs start out to achieve in the first place. This creates additional pressure and stress, which then spreads throughout the workplace environment and leads to a downward spiral. Understanding the Eisenhower Matrix and using it as a business tool for effective delegation and time management can lead to the business running smoothly and provide opportunity for growth and greater freedom for the CEO.

9. Time Management

Managing your time effectively is closely linked to delegation. In order to leverage your time effectively, it requires delegating responsibility for some tasks and areas of the business to someone else or outsourcing them.

Identifying who you can delegate tasks to, allows you to concentrate on the tasks that really matter such as profitability, growth, systems, automation, customer satisfaction, new products and the overall sustainability of the business.

All successful high-performance people understand how important it is to have systems in place to manage their time. This generally involves breaking your time into small blocks. If you are new to a time management system this could initially be 30-minute blocks and then as your understanding, efficiency and discipline improves, the blocks can be gradually reduced to 5-minute blocks.

10. Problem Solving

In any business, it is inevitable that there will be problems to deal with on a regular basis. In order to deal with problems in a timely and efficient manner, it is important to have or develop good problem-solving skills. Sometimes problems will need to be dealt with whilst working under pressure, which is where developing problem-solving skills, strengths and tools are important. It is never the size of our problems that is the problem – it is only ever the size of us and our ability to handle them.

11. Networking

It is frequently said that our Network = our Networth, which can certainly be true. However, it is not the size of our network but the quality of the people within it that will provide you with the best opportunities to grow, offer value and feel supported in the process. I see a lot of people making the mistake of thinking that it is the size of their network that counts and boasting about large social media followings, which do nothing except serve the ego. One person that you have established a real connection with is worth hundreds of virtual connections who are merely unknown names and numbers.

Networking is a low-cost and effective marketing method that can help establish mutually-beneficial relationships with other businesses or individuals. However, not all business owners feel comfortable with networking. So, why do some people shy away and avoid networking?

Here is what I have found the top reasons to be:

- **They lack confidence**
    - Most people fear being rejected, and this is particularly true for some who are new to networking. They may feel intimidated by experienced and confident networkers who appear to make connections easily.

- **They are too busy**
    - If you want to grow your business, you need to make networking part of it.
    - Networking does not have to take a long time. We all have limitations with time, money, and energy. So, it is important to work within these limitations when developing a networking plan. Good networkers give without expectation and they end up getting much more back in return.

- **They think business networking is selling**
  - Some people believe that networking is the same as selling, and this scares them off.
  - Networking is not really marketing or selling but it is part of your marketing and selling process.
  - It is about having conversations that can lead to connections and business relationships.
  - When you introduce yourself to someone and ask to do business with them, that is not networking. That is direct selling. If you have a LinkedIn profile and use the site for making connections (which I highly recommend that you do), you will receive first messages from people you don't know who go straight into direct selling. This is equal to making a marriage proposal to someone you have just met and don't know. There is nothing more off-putting and it could kill any future opportunity that might have been there.
  - With networking, you are connecting with people to build up a relationship where you may do something with them in the future. People are much more likely to do business with you once they get to know you first.

If you think that you don't like networking, here are a few tips to make it enjoyable:

- Attend seminars or social events that do not focus on networking.
- Go to events that are of interest to you.
- Attend events that excite you.
- Bring a friend.
- Prepare questions and topics for conversation.
- Show genuine interest in people you connect with.
- Connect with people you meet on social media.

Networking involves building and cultivating relationships with different people. It is a give and take process. It is all about creating value for your connections. When you focus on how you can help people within your network, you will find them responding to you in the same way.

12 Risk Taking

Business comes with risk. The ability to make well-calculated decisions is what differentiates a great leader from a good one. Everyone has their own level of risk. Having too low or high a risk level can both be equally harmful to the survival and growth of a company. It is all about developing a balanced and healthy attitude towards risk and developing strategies that stack the odds in your favour.

A business owner should be daring enough to take some risks, whilst also having contingencies in place to cover the downside. Small companies make small moves, big companies make big moves.

13 Managing Stress

One of the most important parts of the entrepreneurial journey is being able to develop the skills and mindset to manage your personal and business life effectively so that stress does not get on top of you.

Stress can be both positive and motivate us, or negative and drain us. The diagram below illustrates the difference between positive and negative stress and how it impacts performance as I referred to earlier in the book.

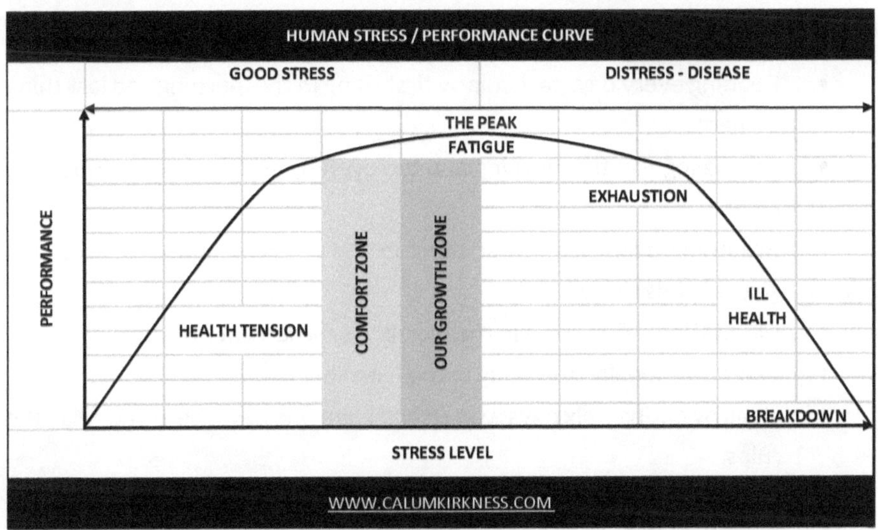

My own journey and health have followed the graph above on several occasions before I finally got the lessons and understood why.

It is only when we take a critical look back at ourselves that we can see the reasons and learn the lessons. It is a law of human nature to keep repeating the same mistakes until we finally learn the lessons that the universe has been trying to communicate and teach us. Our body, mind and spirit are always communicating a message to us to keep us on the right track, but we are taught to think logically and allow our social programming and ego to take over from our intuition and gut feeling, which is never a good thing.

To have a successful business, you need to have a stress-free and healthy home life and to have a successful and healthy home life, you need to have a stress-free and healthy business. When we look around us, we can easily identify and see this to be the case.

It is almost impossible to have a totally stress-free life, but it is essential to have the right tools and strategies in place and have the capacity to be able to manage the stress effectively. One of the ways to have a healthy, balanced life is to develop a healthy morning routine and have effective time management and delegation systems in place, which virtually all successful people do.

Here are a few things that can help you to manage stress:

- Practising gratitude first thing in the morning and last thing at night.
- Reading every day, particularly first thing in the morning and last thing at night.
- Journaling – in the morning and the evening and if you wake up in the night.
- Breathing exercises – first thing in the morning and when you feel stress levels rising.
- Meditation – first thing in the morning or when out in nature.
- Exercise – ideally first thing in the morning.
- Healthy eating – six days a week and have one day where you relax the rules.
- Spending time alone – set aside some time for this every day.
- Spending time in nature – ideally daily.

- Spending time with positive people – make this a habit as much as possible.
- Avoid negative people – avoid them as much as possible.
- Time management systems – have time allocated for work, rest, reflection and play.
- Effective delegation system – delegate as much as possible, but not everything.

Emotional Intelligence

Emotional intelligence is now seen as the number one indicator of success as an entrepreneur.

You don't have to be the smartest person in the world to be the most successful and more and more people are now noticing it. People with average IQs often tend to perform better in business and the workplace than with high-IQs, which is making emotional intelligence a much sought-after quality to have in the workplace and is an extremely useful skill for entrepreneurs to have.

How Can Emotional Intelligence Make Entrepreneurs More Successful?

Improved self-awareness

Knowing where you stand emotionally and being able to identify your emotions, strengths, and weaknesses, and how they affect others is important when dealing with any situation. When you learn to evaluate your emotions, you can manage and express them in a healthy and helpful manner, which can act as a buffer against your emotions building up and distorting your perception. Improving your emotional intelligence can help you make better decisions, which leads to better outcomes.

Self-regulation

Most of the time you will have no control over when you experience certain emotions such as anger or anxiety. However, you can control or redirect disruptive emotions and adapt to changes. People with high EI do other activities such as take long walks, meditate, or pray, which can all help to direct energy in a positive way.

More effective communication

It is difficult to have a deep conversation with someone if you cannot empathise and identify with their emotions. Communication becomes much more difficult and less effective. Entrepreneurs who have high emotional intelligence can leverage the skill and use empathy, problem-solving, and social skills to create strong relationships and develop solutions.

Control of emotions

Entrepreneurship is no walk in the park and there will be many roadblocks on the path to success. As a business owner, you will have to deal with everything including: angry or difficult customers and clients, difficult conversations, disappointing results or product launches, etc. We can't control everything that happens, but with high emotional intelligence, we can acknowledge our emotions and deal with difficult situations without erupting or suppressing our emotions. If we don't do this, they will only erupt later at an inappropriate time or, worse still, the repressed emotion will remain stuck inside and later manifest as illness affecting your health.

Identifying customer needs

Understanding what is in your customer's mind can be trickier than you might think. Making assumptions is a dangerous and misleading route to take. The best way to identify customer needs is to use a combination of data and direct communication about their experiences. When you can empathise with your customers, you can better identify and understand where you can improve and better meet their needs, which is also useful information that can help you market your products and services more effectively.

Unifying the team through enhanced leadership

Even if you are very early in the start-up stage of building a business, you're probably thinking ahead to when you will have a team working for you. Emotionally intelligent leaders bring out the best in their employees, which is the foundation for cultivating respect, a unified vision and good morale, which leads to improved productivity. Improving emotional intelligence can be difficult, but it is possible as long as you have an open mind and a willingness to put in some tough work.

Some Steps You Can Take To Improve Your Emotional Intelligence

1. Read books on personal development and business

90% of top performers have above-average emotional intelligence, and many of them have written books. Reading about the success that others have had can show you what steps you need to take in order to reach your goals.

2. Listen and practise empathy

Practise empathy during conversations with colleagues, friends, and family. Really listen to what is being said and think about what the other person might be thinking and feeling. Most people listen to reply – without taking the time to understand what is really being said and felt.

3. Talk to a coach

Developing emotional intelligence can be challenging. One of the most difficult aspects of improving emotional intelligence is that it is hard to do on our own and measure how well we are making progress. Having a coach to give you benchmarks, provide accountability and assess how you're doing on an ongoing basis means you will be much more likely to make progress and succeed at the highest level.

Key Aspects Of Emotional Intelligence And How To Identify It In Others:

- Motivation.
- Drive for excellence.
- Commitment.
- Initiative.
- Optimism.
- Empathy.
- Rendering service.
- Developing subordinates.
- Leveraging diversity.

- Political astuteness.
- Focusing on and understanding needs.
- Social skills.
- Influencer.
- Excellent communicator.
- Effective leader.
- Change catalyst.
- Effective at conflict management.
- Relationship builder.
- Collaborator and co-operator.
- Team player.
- Calm under pressure.
- Leads by example.
- Puts consideration into making business decisions.
- Has a work-life balance.
- Welcomes change.
- Focused on their tasks.
- Not a perfectionist.
- Identifies their strengths and weaknesses.
- Doesn't dwell on the past.
- Maintains a positive outlook on life.
- Knows how to set boundaries.

You can see from this section how emotional intelligence is very closely linked to customer service and why it plays such an important factor in the success of a business. Without customers, a business does not exist. It is also important to consider the satisfaction of the employees within the business as without them a business would not be able to grow. When a happy employee meets a happy customer during a transaction in your business, you know you are on the right track.

Transparency

Building a successful business requires transparency with your team on the things that both directly and indirectly affect them. Open transparency involves sharing both the good and the bad things and disclosing the risks involved.

Discussing your own apprehensions with the team always leads to ground-breaking solutions to even the toughest of challenges and biggest of problems. A lack of transparency can result in ambiguity, confusion, dissatisfaction, frustration and loss of morale, which can lead to resentment and rumours circulating, which are all bad for business.

"Our business will only ever be as strong
as the weakest link."
– Calum Kirkness

Now that we have looked at the essential skills, let's have a closer look at doing your SWOT analysis.

What Is SWOT Analysis?

A SWOT analysis is a simple yet powerful tool, which is effective in helping to develop your business plan and strategies. It works at any time whether you are at start-up stage or reviewing and building up an existing company.

SWOT stands for Strengths, Weaknesses, Opportunities and Threats.

Strengths and weaknesses are internal to your company and are things that you have some control over and can change. For example: the people on your team, your products, your services, intellectual property, your location, etc.

Opportunities and threats are external to your company and are things that you have little control over. You can take advantage of opportunities and protect against threats, but you can't change them. Examples include: competitors, price of raw materials, customer shopping trends, economy.

A SWOT analysis organises your top strengths, weaknesses, opportunities and threats into an organized list, which is usually presented in a simple two-by-two grid layout as shown in the example below:

SWOT ANALYSIS		
	HELPFUL	**HARMFUL**
INTERNAL	**STRENGTHS**	**WEAKNESSES**
EXTERNAL	**OPPORTUNTIES**	**THREATS**

For new business start-ups, a SWOT analysis is part of the business planning process and will help you clarify a strategy to start on the right footing and know the direction that you need to take.

For existing businesses, a SWOT analysis can be used to assess the current situation and help determine a strategy to move forward. It is a good idea to carry out a new SWOT analysis every time there is rumour of a new competition or every three, six to twelve months depending on how quickly the company is growing or the company and economy is changing. For example, if a new competitor enters the market by surprise or there is a shock event that hits the economy, it can be a good idea to review the company's strengths, weaknesses, opportunities and threats.

Negative changes are generally viewed as a disaster by most and the media will do everything to fuel and spread the negative news, but these situations can provide some of the best opportunities for entrepreneurs. It is said that more millionaires are created in a downturn than when the economy is booming ahead.

For a SWOT analysis to be fully effective, all the company founders and leaders need to be involved. However, to get the best results, it is helpful to gather a group of people from different disciplines who can offer a wide and varied range of perspective on the company. Everyone should have a place at the table.

Innovative companies will also look outside their company when they perform a SWOT analysis to get input from customers and the public.

If you are starting or running a business on your own, you can still do a SWOT analysis by obtaining the views from friends, suppliers and your wider network, who know you and your business. It is important to bear in mind, that their feedback may be flawed and does require careful consideration. Some of them may be scared to speak the truth, particularly on your weaknesses, and hold back valuable feedback that would be helpful, whilst others may provide deliberately misleading information based on jealousy, etc. The key is to have lots of different points of view and then take an overall objective view of the feedback.

Never take criticism from people that you would not go to for advice, unless they are also a customer. It is rarely a good idea to only have the feedback of friends.

Here is an example of how you could go about doing a SWOT analysis.

Give people prior notification that you are carrying out the SWOT analysis and give them time to think about the four different areas that you would like their feedback and input on.

Provide everyone with a form where they can type in up to 10 items in each category, with a sealed box where they can place their completed form anonymously ahead of the meeting to discuss the SWOT analysis. This prevents group-think, people worrying about whether their handwriting will be recognised and their feedback judged, and ensures that all voices are heard.

Prepare the results of the SWOT into a report format where all the feedback results are recorded and distribute this ahead of the meeting. During the meeting, allow everyone around the table to provide their views and feedback by giving everyone a few minutes to have their say. Have time limits to give everyone equal opportunity. Time limits also help people to concentrate their minds and keep the meeting productive.

Doing a SWOT analysis is like having a brainstorming meeting. After the private brainstorming session and before the end of the meeting, it is time to rank the ideas. Someone in the room should be able to make the final call on the priorities. This is usually the CEO, but it could be delegated to someone else in charge of business strategy.

Here are some questions that can help inspire your SWOT analysis:

Strengths

- What business product, processes and systems are working well and are profitable?
- What assets do you have in your team, such as knowledge, education, skills, reputation, awards and network?
- What physical and non-physical assets do you have, such as property, customers, equipment, technology, cash, and intellectual property such as trademarks and patents?
- What advantages do you have over your competitors?

Weaknesses

- Are there gaps in the team and/or supply chain?
- Are there business products, processes and systems that need to be improved?
- Are there assets that your company needs more of, such as property, money or plant and equipment, patent protection?
- Is your location suitable or holding back growth and success?

Opportunities

- Is your market sector growing and are there trends that will encourage people to buy more of the products and services that you are selling?
- Are there any upcoming events that your company may be able to take advantage of to grow your business?

- Are there upcoming changes to regulations that might impact your company positively?
- Do your customers think highly of you?

Threats

- Are there potential competitors who may enter your market?
- Is your supply chain strong? Are they able to supply the raw materials in the quantity and at the prices you need?
- Could developments in technology change how you do business?
- Is the economy and consumer behaviour changing and could this negatively impact your business?

What To Do Next

You can use the analysis to produce a list of actions that you can take which can be included in your business plan to work on during the next few months.

It is important to look at how:

- Your strengths can be used to capitalise on the opportunities.
- Your strengths can be used to minimise any threats.
- Your strengths can be used to reduce any weaknesses.
- Your strengths can be increased further through opportunities.

With your goals and actions in hand, you will be a long way towards completing a strategic plan for your business.

Your level of success is determined by your level of strength, discipline and perseverance. It is therefore important to use your strengths and natural skills to build your brand and reputation, and to hire experts to do what you are weak in and do not enjoy.

Use your stories to be authentic about your strengths and weaknesses. Authenticity is seen as a great way to build connections but does require a degree of caution also, particularly when it affects customers. It takes years to build a great brand and reputation and minutes to destroy it. I share about a good example of this and look at branding and standing out from the crowd in a later in this book.

CHAPTER 5

STRUCTURES

In this chapter, we will look at different types of company structures. Namely:

- Legal Structures
- Management & Operational Structures

1. Selecting the Right Legal Structure

Choosing the best legal structure for your business is a complex area. I would recommend that you always obtain professional advice from specialist tax and financial experts and accountants. Having the wrong structure can have significant tax and legal implications.

I am not a tax, financial or accountancy advisor or expert. So this section contains only basic information of the main options available and what is involved. This should give you an idea of what to do further research on and what your tax and financial advisors and accountant will discuss with you when they are helping you choose the best option for your individual circumstances.

The most popular types of company legal structures are:

- Individual sole trader.
- Private company limited by shares.
- Private company limited by guarantee.
- Limited liability partnership (LLP).

Individual Sole Trader

Setting up as a sole trader is one of the easiest things to do in terms of registration and administration requirements. However, there is no legal distinction between the business and the individual owner, which means you are personally responsible for all business debts with no limit on liability. Your home and other assets may be at risk if you are unable to meet your financial obligations. On the positive side, as there is no legal distinction between your personal finances and business finances, there is no need to go through any complex procedures to remove money for personal use, which can be a benefit.

You will be responsible to register with HMRC and prepare a Self-Assessment Tax Return to report your annual income and tax liability and pay Income Tax and National Insurance on your earnings at the end of every tax year. Unless this is an area that you already have knowledge of, I recommend that you get an accountant to do this for you.

Limited Company

A limited company is one of the most popular business structures for all sizes of organisation. This is due to some benefits that it provides over other types of legal business structures.

Limited companies must be incorporated at Companies House. There is more ownership flexibility with this type of business structure, and they can be owned and operated by an individual or multiple people.

A limited company exists as a legal 'person'. This means it is responsible for its own liabilities. The owners of a company are protected by limited liability and not personally liable for business debts, other than what they agree to contribute and guarantee to the business.

Limited companies are often more tax-efficient than sole trader businesses. A company limited by shares is most suitable if you want to keep business profits for yourself. A limited by guarantee structure is better suited to non-profit businesses and charitable enterprises.

An overview of some of the advantages and disadvantages of forming a limited company, compared to trading as an individual sole trader are listed below.

Advantages of trading as a limited company:

The main reasons for incorporating and trading as limited company are limited liability, tax efficiency and professional status.

- Minimising personal liability.
- Separate legal identity.
- Professional status.
- Credibility and trust.
- Tax efficiency and planning.
- Higher personal remuneration.
- Splitting income.
- Investment and lending opportunities.
- Protecting a company name.
- Easier to sell/transfer business ownership.
- May be easier to access finance.
- Pension.

Disadvantages of a limited company:

As you would expect with anything that provides many benefits, there are also some disadvantages:

- Must be officially incorporated at Companies House.
- Company name is subject to certain restrictions.
- Not suitable for undischarged bankrupts or disqualified directors.
- Required to disclose personal and corporate information on public record.
- More complex and time-consuming accounting requirements.
- Likely need to appoint an accountant to help you with your tax affairs.
- Strict procedures for withdrawing money from the business.
- A confirmation statement and annual accounts must be filed at Companies House each year.
- Must send a company tax return and annual accounts to HMRC every year.
- Must adhere to strict record-keeping requirements.
- A number of company registers and records must be maintained and made available for public inspection at your registered office.
- If you make any changes to your company details, you must notify Companies House immediately.

Limited Liability Partnership

- LLP for short is a popular structure for firms of lawyers, accountants, architects, and other types of professionals who run a partnership with other people of the same or complementary profession. There need to be at least two people to set up an LLP. This type of business structure is very similar to a normal partnership in terms of ownership structure and taxation, but it provides limited liability to all partners.

Deciding Whether To Trade As An Individual, Limited Company or Partnership.

- There are advantages and disadvantages to each structure, which will depend on everyone's individual circumstances.
- Do not listen to anyone who says there is a one-size-fits-all strategy. Seek out the best advice, as this area can have a big impact on your profits and financial wealth.

Main Factors To Consider When Choosing The Best Structure For You:

- What is your current personal tax situation?
- What are your future goals?
- What allowances will you be able to claim?
- What expenses will you be able to claim?
- Could you spread your tax liability through other people?
- What is your risk profile?
- How will the taxman view your status based on your choices?
- Will you need to be VAT registered?
- What is your financial strategy?
- How will you mitigate or reduce income tax, capital gains tax, inheritance tax, stamp duty, corporation tax?

Limited companies and LLPs share some similarities, the main one being the reduced financial responsibility of the owners. However, they do have significant differences as well, namely:

- Capital investment opportunities.

- Flexibility of internal structure and members' rights.
- The allocation and taxation of business profits.

Choosing the most appropriate legal structure will depend entirely upon the kind of business you are planning to have in the future or currently have.

A company limited by shares is the most popular structure for profit-making businesses. A limited company structure is also best if you plan to employ lots of people and/or you want the option of selling shares in your business to raise capital investment. It is also a more tax-efficient structure for many types of businesses.

A company limited by guarantee is the best option for non-profit organisations.

An LLP can be best suited to meet the needs of certain professionals who usually form traditional partnerships, such as solicitors, doctors, accountants and architects.

LLPs provide the same benefits as traditional partnerships, with the added advantage of reduced financial responsibility for the partners. An LLP structure is also good for businesses with minimal employees (if any) and only a few partners, each of whom make similar contributions to the business, enjoy equal rights and responsibilities, and take a similar share of business profits.

The main differences between a limited company and an LLP

- A limited company can be registered, owned and managed by just one individual. One person can act as both the director and shareholder (or guarantor). A minimum of two members are required to set up an LLP. However, one way around this is maybe to set up a dormant limited company as the second LLP member.
- The liability of company shareholders or guarantors is limited to the amount paid or unpaid on their shares, or the amount of their guarantees. The liability of LLP members is limited to the amount each member guarantees to pay if the business runs into financial difficulty or is wound up.
- A limited company can receive loans and capital investment from

outside investors. An LLP can only receive loan capital. It cannot offer equity shares in the business to non-LLP members.

- Limited companies pay Corporation Tax and Capital Gains Tax (CGT) on all taxable income. In an LLP the members pay Income Tax, National Insurance and CGT on all taxable income. The LLP itself has no tax liability.
- It is easier to change the internal management structure and distribution of profits in an LLP.
- A limited company can be operated as a non-profit business. An LLP must be set up with the intention of making a profit.

Internal structure and allocation of profits

An LLP can offer greater flexibility than a limited company in terms of altering the rights, duties and profit entitlement of individual members. Such arrangements can be agreed verbally amongst LLP members, and they can be quickly and easily changed at any time. However, it is commonplace to draw up an LLP Agreement. This document will outline the internal management structure of the business and the various arrangements in place, thus avoiding or at least minimising the potential for internal conflict and disputes.

The voting rights and profit entitlement of shareholders are governed by the prescribed particulars attached to their shares. In most instances, companies will issue just one type of share, thus providing equal rights and profit entitlement to all shareholders.

It is more difficult to change the rights and profit entitlement of shareholders because they are stipulated in these prescribed particulars. Most companies will draw up a shareholders' agreement to outline their rights, responsibilities and duties, and the way in which the company should operate.

TAX AND FINANCIALS

Business Taxation

The following section is a beginner's guide to business tax. Taxation is a complex subject and varies depending on everyone's individual circumstances, which is why it is important to get expert advice from a specialist tax advisor and accountant in your chosen field of business before starting out. Or, if you have already started, it is essential to understand what options you have to minimise tax to your short-, medium- and long-term benefit.

There are six main categories of taxes that can affect business depending on the structure:

1. Income Tax.
2. National Insurance Contributions (NIC).
3. Capital Gains Tax (CGT). Applies to Sole Traders and not Limited Companies.
4. Stamp Duty Land Tax (SDLT).
5. Inheritance Tax.
6. Corporation Tax.

There are also several tax allowances that apply in certain circumstances. Having knowledge of these and applying them is where a specialist expert accountant and tax advisor can earn their worth.

The taxes you pay and the allowances that you can apply will depend on which type of structure you use to invest and trade in.

Types of taxation that may apply when trading as an individual sole trader:

- Income Tax.
- National Insurance.
- Capital Gains Tax.
- Stamp Duty.
- Additional Stamp Duty.
- Inheritance Tax.
- VAT – if registered and company turnover exceeds the HMRC limit.

Types of taxation that may apply when trading as a Ltd company:

- Corporation Tax.
- National Insurance Taxes related to employment (If applicable).
- Stamp Duty.

- Additional Stamp Duty – if buying property.
- VAT – if registered and company turnover exceeds the HMRC limit.

Different Tax Liabilities Of LLPs And Limited Companies

Limited company tax liability

All taxable income generated by a limited company is subject to corporation tax. Any salary a director receives will be liable for Income Tax, National Insurance and employer's NI. However, directors are often also shareholders. This means they are treated as employees of their own company. The distribution of profits to directors can be done in such a way that much of the money they receive is not subject to Corporation Tax or personal Income Tax.

By paying a director a salary of no more than their tax-free personal allowance, and distributing additional profits by way of shareholder dividends, a director can legally minimise their personal tax liability. Dividends are paid from post-tax profits and a percentage of the payments are currently tax-free. Additional dividend income is taxed according to the tax bracket of the recipient.

Tax efficiency – leaving money in the business

In instances where you will make more annual profit than you need to take out of your business, a limited company will be more tax efficient. There is no need to withdraw all surplus income immediately. Instead, you could leave some of the profits in the business and defer tax by withdrawing the surplus in a future tax year.

This is not possible with an LLP. Regardless of whether the members take all their annual profit entitlement or leave some in the business, all profit is subject to Income Tax in the financial year it is generated.

Before you start trading, it is important to get expert advice on which structure will be the most tax efficient and beneficial for you in reaching your investment, financial and wealth goals.

2. Company Management and Operational Structures

Management structures are generally referred to as either flat or tall and there is everything in between. In order to create a company that has the potential to upset an existing industry and create a lasting impact on the world, your corporate structure and culture must be unique, inspiring and challenging.

Where there are many levels in the management hierarchy, the organisation is said to be 'tall'. This will tend to result in the members of the team having narrow spans of control. Whereas when there are just a small number of levels in the hierarchy, the organisation is said to be 'flat'. Flat organisations will tend to have wide spans of control for the team members.

The diagram below gives a basic illustration of how the two different organisational structures might look with the same number of people:

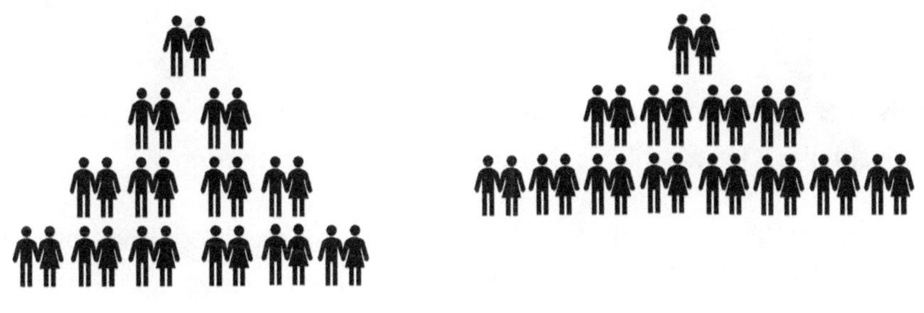

Tall Structure   Flat Sturcture

One of the reasons why big companies fail is that they focus too much on committees and internal politics, which creates lots of bureaucracy. This results in losing focus and sight of the unique value that their product and services bring to the consumer, which tends to lead to the customer experience becoming more complex.

In order to provide the best experience, customer-facing members of the team need to have the authority to act quickly when faced with a dissatisfied customer in order to save the relationship.

When things go wrong, or a customer perceives an issue, your repeat business from that person is put in serious jeopardy. It is not the problem but how the company reacts and handles the issue that will determine whether the relationship is damaged or saved – and, more importantly, saved and maintained at the level that it was at before the issue. Quite often, a customer's perception of the company will be raised if the situation is handled well.

In a bureaucracy, the decision to fix a customer issue, and the steps involved rapidly multiply, which means that it takes longer for the customer issue to be resolved if at all.

In a flatter organisational chart, employees can empower themselves, or immediately gain one-time authority from a superior to take care of the customer, which can lead to a boost in staff morale, as well as dealing with and achieving customer satisfaction much earlier. The longer a situation is left, the unhappier the customer will tend to get, which also means their dissatisfaction has more time to spread to family, friends, colleagues, fellow professionals and everyone on their social media, etc. Bad news travels much further and faster than good news.

Whilst flat organisations have many advantages, they can also have their disadvantages. One of which is that they can be too fast to control.

For example: think about the last time you went to a fast food drive-thru and ordered a calorie-laden burger with fries and drink. If there was just you or you and your friend, the decision would be easy (even if it is not the right one)! But if you were running a health and fitness company and you had a company executive, a member of the nutritional advisory panel, and the manager of health and fitness with you in the car, the decision to eat something that is bad for your health would have likely been blocked by the wisdom and self-control of the organisation.

With flat organisational structures, there is less oversight and outside input on decision making, which can provide a quick solution that feels good at the time, but is not the right or best decision in the longer term.

The challenge with a flat leadership structure is in balancing the need for oversight with the need for speed and efficiency.

The Bureaucracy of Tall Structures Gives Executives More Control Over The Brand and Customer Experience

The impact of a wise, talented executive team can be more fully felt in a tall organisational structure.

The thoughts and decisions of executive management can be communicated to mid-level management, who can then reach out to supervisors and carefully make sure the management vision is followed. However, with each layer of communication, there is the risk that the message gets misunderstood, misinterpreted and manipulated. This can be very frustrating for executives leading a company or organisation.

For a flat organisation to execute the vision of a founder or the executive committee reliably, the organisation needs to be relatively small and easy for a founder or leader to oversee the entire operation.

Depending on the energy level of the leadership team, it may be easier to run things through bureaucratic channels. A high-energy team could get the same quality of execution in a flatter structure, but the risk of a failure in proper execution is higher.

In tall organisations, managers have smaller spans of control (i.e. fewer people reporting directly to them). This reduces the number of people they must manage, but means it takes longer for information to travel through the layers of the organisation.

In recent years, tall organisations have tended to be associated with large bureaucracies. Communication will be formal and middle managers may be able to use information as a device to retain control. On the other hand, smaller spans of control may mean that managers have more time to manage.

Is There Such A Thing As The Perfect Organisation Structure For Every Business?

Part of the excitement and beauty of building a new business, or rearranging an existing structure to accomplish a goal, is that you are free to experiment. Trying different structures has the potential for both financial loss and reward, but trying new things is what entrepreneurial spirit is made of and makes it so resilient even in the toughest of economic times.

By focusing on the core competencies and strengths of the company and the employees, and then empowering them to use those strengths, is what creates a great company. You'll be surprised at how powerful a team can be when they are unshackled from restrictive processes and chains of command. To achieve this, there needs to be clear leadership, but if you hire the right people, you will simply need to point the ship in the right direction and everyone will pull together on the oars to build a company whose products and services lead and are difficult to compete with. Having a team of enthusiastic, energised, talented people with defined areas of responsibility can minimise the need for unnecessary layers of bureaucracy. Remember, that finding people as passionate about a product or service as its founder is rare.

What To Do When An Organisation Begins To Get Too Many Layers

This tends to happen during periods of rapid growth or over time if there are no systems in place to regularly review everything the company does with a view to maintaining maximum simplicity, efficiency and customer and employee satisfaction.

In recent years, there has been a trend where tall organisations have tended to become flatter by removing various levels in the hierarchy. This process is regularly referred to as delayering which has been facilitated by:

- **Information technology**, which has reduced the need for many middle management jobs, which were largely concerned with processing information to facilitate control within the organisational hierarchy.

- **Empowerment**, the management philosophy of empowerment, where people at lower levels have been delegated authority to take actions and make decisions which would previously have been the domain of middle manager. Training plays an important part in this.

Advantages of Delayering

- Reduction in costs as middle managers' salary costs are removed.

- Increased levels of motivation and performance as people at lower levels are given more power/discretion to make decisions.
- Improved, faster communication between senior management and operational levels, which is becoming increasingly important in a fast-changing, uncertain and increasingly competitive external environment.

Disadvantages of Delayering

- A possible loss of control.
- Middle managers are often necessary to translate the inevitably broad and general plans of senior management into operational plans and actions that can be implemented.
- Senior managers may have a blurred understanding of what is going on at the operational level, which means that more is entrusted to relatively junior people.

CHAPTER 6

START-UP

Starting up your own business is a big commitment, so it's important that you fully understand your reasons for wanting to start the business along with understanding the key components of a business and what makes some businesses succeed whilst others fail. When you understand these three areas, you can significantly increase your chances of success.

Fully Understand Your Reasons For Starting Your Business

The six following questions can be useful in establishing why you want to do what you do and where you want to take your business, which are your mission and your vision:

- ✓ Why do you want to do it? (Your why and purpose).
- ✓ Who are you now and who do you need to become? (Your reality / personal development).
- ✓ What do you want to be known for? (Your personal and business branding).
- ✓ Where you are now? (Your current location / circumstances).
- ✓ Where do you want to be? (Your ideal destination / lifestyle).
- ✓ When do you want to get there? (Your arrival time).

By setting out your answers to the questions above on one side of a sheet of paper, it can provide greater clarity on your goals, the reasons why you want to start a business, your business idea and solution.

5 Key Components Of A Business:

- Idea / Solution
- Team
- Timing
- Business Model
- Funding

Here Are The Top 5 Reasons Why Businesses Fail (In Order From Most To Least):

- **Timing** – This is the biggest factor when it comes to success or failure in any business. Think back to the examples I shared earlier in the book regarding my grandfather's idea to purchase the wooden military buildings and carve them up into house-size sections to provide affordable housing. The idea, solution and timing were perfect: the timber buildings were available for sale, there was a shortage of accommodation and people didn't have much money. However, when my father later purchased some more of the buildings years later, the results were very different. Another example would be my grandparents' timing in selling the land on the small island just before a large oil company wanted to buy it.

  A more recent example would be Airbnb. When it started, people questioned whether it would work based on whether people would allow strangers into their homes, but the timing was perfect as it was just after the economy collapsed and homeowners needed additional income and people who needed the accommodation wanted cheaper rates. Had Airbnb launched one or two years earlier, the business might have failed, and the idea might never have been implemented again due to the belief that it was flawed and would not work.

  As I mentioned earlier in the book, ideas have a shelf life and it's important to recognise when the expiry date has been reached and adapt to the new market conditions and trends. As part of your exit strategy planning, you may wish to consider the anticipated shelf life of your idea and sell the company when it's at its peak.

- **Team / Execution** – Business is a people game that comes down to good teamwork. In order to succeed, the team needs to have the right mindset, a good network, rapport, relationships and reputation. People do business with people that they know, like and trust.

- **Idea** – Whilst I would say the single most important component of a business is the idea, it is not the number 1 reason a business will fail.

- **Business Model** – A business can start without a business model; this can be added later. It is said that YouTube started out without any business model. The business model needs to be adaptable.

- **Funding** – Whilst funding is crucial to starting up and operating a business, it is the lowest ranking reason of the five when it comes to reasons for failure. A great idea that is timed right and executed by a good team based on a solid model will always be able to access funding. There is a huge amount of money circulating the world every day looking for a good home that will provide an attractive return.

Starting a new business can be very exciting, particularly when you have found something that you are passionate about. I believe that we all have an INNER GPS (our intuition), which I call my GENIUS POSITIONING SYSTEM, which is always guiding us.

A dream can feel like it is unachievable because you do not have all the answers, and this is where faith and listening to your intuition is important. If you can dream it, you can achieve it! Without some sort of a plan of action, a dream remains just a dream. To achieve our dreams, we need to set some goals. A goal is a dream with a deadline. If we are to achieve our goals, we must take action – and the best way to do this is to develop a plan of action that will help us achieve the goals and dreams that we desire.

The Importance Of Goal Setting and Planning

Studies have demonstrated the importance of goal setting and planning.

There was a study carried out by Harvard MBA Business School on the class of 1979 into the effectiveness of goal setting and having a plan. The results clearly demonstrate the importance of having a written plan in place.

Prior to graduation, it was determined that:

- 84% of the students had set no goals at all.
- 13% of the students had set written goals but had no concrete plans.
- 3% of the class had both written goals and concrete plans.

The results 10 years later:

- The 13% of the class that had set written goals, but had not created plans, were making twice as much money as the 84% of the class that had set no goals at all.

- The 3% of the class that had written goals and a plan, were making ten times as much as the rest of the 97% of the class.

Some figures that you can find on the Internet regarding goals set as part of New Year's resolutions, claim that only 8% to 9% of people achieve their resolutions, which means that 91 to 92% of people fail.

It's clearly important to figure out what motivates you or, more importantly, what inspires you if you want to achieve your business goals. Below is a list of eight common motivators that people have. Everyone will have a unique set of motivators. However, the less you focus on satisfying the ego, and the more you focus on the customer and providing value for them, the more successful you will tend to be:

1. **Recognition**
   You feel energised by public admiration and praise. If this is you, then the fear of letting someone else down motivates you to push forward. It's a good strategy if you have a coach and accountability partner.

2. **Challenge**
   You feel energised by finding creative solutions for difficult situations that others can't. This can be a good sign that you're motivated to set yourself up for success.

3. **Growth**
   You feel energised when you are learning, so you look out for and take opportunities to develop yourself.

4. **Career progression**
   You get satisfaction from building your responsibilities at work and progressing up the career ladder.

5. **Money**
   You feel energised by working hard to earn bonuses, commissions, or financial rewards.

6. **Making a difference**
   You experience a sense of peace, happiness, and meaning when you

work to improve the lives of others or contribute to society.

7. **Incentives**

   You love the thrill of competitive activities and enjoy earning prizes associated with success.

8. **Work-life balance**

   You enjoy having flexibility and balance in your life.

When you are setting goals and creating plans, it is important to check in with your gut feeling and intuition and check if they are really what inspires you and what you want.

I find a good system for setting objectives is to use a mnemonic called SMART goals. SMART is an acronym for:

- **S**pecific
- **M**easurable
- **A**ttainable
- **R**ealistic
- **T**ime-bound

"When we fail to plan, we are planning to fail by default."
– Calum Kirkness

There is more information on setting goals and developing a success mindset in Chapter 17.

Preparing Your Business Plan

Preparing a traditional business plan for your start-up, or next phase of business growth, can be a daunting and overwhelming challenge that can lead to paralysis by analysis. It doesn't need to be that way, and this chapter is designed to help you identify the key areas of information required for you to put together a good business plan. Thinking alone will not provide the clarity on your idea. It will come from putting pen to paper and acting on the information on the key areas and the clarity will develop from there.

For a business plan to be effective, it needs to be accurate, concise, simple and easy to understand. It's also important that you can clearly convey the information to others in a form that is understandable to them, particularly if you are pitching to potential investors. There is a saying that, "if you confuse them, you lose them." The same is true for your business plan. The quality of information in the plan is much more important than the quantity of information.

> *"The quality of information in a plan is much more important than the quantity of information."*
> **– Calum Kirkness**

Over the years, I have developed some techniques to help me whenever I am preparing a business plan. One is a lean planning technique, where the plan initially gets mapped out on a single sheet of paper. It's effectively a mind map of your business. Having a visual image of all the parts of a business on one sheet, and seeing how they interlink, can help clarify things. This can also give you the inspiration to then come up with further appropriate and key content to include in your full business plan that will give others a detailed understanding of your plan. You want people to read your plan, so it needs to be concise and crystal clear. I suggest 20 pages is generally a good size.

> *"Most things in life are simple when you know how, but that doesn't make them easy."*
> **– Calum Kirkness**

There are 3 basic rules for writing a business plan:

1. Keep it short

- First, start with your one-page lean business plan.
- Second, keep it concise, precise, simple and easy to understand.
- Third, you want the reader to feel interested. Make it visually attractive and exciting to read.
- Fourth, your business plan should be a tool that you use to run and grow your business, which you continue to use and refine over time. If the plan isn't working, change the plan, not the goal.

2. Know your audience

- Write your plan in plain and easy language that is appealing to your audience and which they will understand. No one is impressed by jargon, the use of fancy words or information that is not relevant to them.

3. Don't be intimidated

- Most business owners and entrepreneurs aren't business experts and don't have degrees in business.
- Writing a business plan may seem like a big hurdle, but it doesn't have to be. You know your business better than anyone and you are the expert on it.

Writing Your Business Plan

A well-thought-out business plan lets JV partners and investors know that you are serious about the business. The seven components that you will normally find in a typical business plan include:

1. Executive Summary
2. Company Description and Vision
3. Marketing Analysis and Plan
4. Organisational Management
5. Sales Strategies
6. Financial Plan
7. Exit Strategy (if applicable)

1. Executive Summary and Mission Statement

The executive summary is the elevator pitch for your business that should spark interest and make investors eager to learn more. The executive summary condenses all the vital information listed below in your business plan into a high-level one- or two-page summary:

- **Overview / Mission Statement** – Your company mission should be short—one or two sentences at most—and should encompass, at a very high level, what you are trying to do.

- **Company Description** – Describe all the key facts on the business.
- **Opportunity** – One or two sentences that summarise the problem that exists and you are solving in the market.
- **Solution** – How your product or service addresses the problem for the customers you have identified in the market.
- **Marketing** – Details of the size of the market, your ideal customer and how you will reach them.
- **Competition** – A brief description of how your target market is solving their problem today. What are the alternatives or substitutes in the market?
- **Team** – Provide a brief overview of your company and team and a short explanation of why you are the right people to take your idea to market.
- **Financial Plan** – A brief summary highlighting the key aspects of your financial plan, ideally with a chart that shows your planned sales, expenses and profitability.
- **Funding Requirements** – If you are writing a business plan to get a bank loan or you are asking angel investors or venture capitalists for funding, include the details of what you need in the executive summary.
- **Milestones and Traction** – Investors will want to see if there has been progress made so far and future milestones that you intend to hit. If you can show that your potential customers are interested in or perhaps already buying your product or service, this is great information to highlight and include.
- **Exit Strategy** – If planned. It is good to have an idea of this even when starting out.

I recommend writing the executive summary last so that you can summarise and include all the essential ideas from other sections. You can also try writing it first and then review and edit it after you have completed the rest of the plan.

2. Company Description and Vision

This section should tell the story about your business idea and goals, and allow others to connect with you. The information that you can give in the company description section includes:

- When you formed your business.

- Company history to date.
- Your vision statement.
- Your values.
- Type of business.
- What is the business model?
- What are your products / services and revenue sources?
- Who are your intended customers?
- Do you have unique business relationships that offer you an advantage?
- Where is the company located?
- Who are the company founding members and owners?
- Organisational chart.
- What is the legal structure?
- What are the legal requirements?
- Intellectual property / patents / trademarks.
- What is the projected growth of the company?
- What are your big goals for the company?

3. Marketing Analysis And Plan

In this section, you can include information on the following:

- **Your market research** – Classic methods of identifying data on different sub-sets for your target market are to use the TAM, SAM and SOM acronyms which are definitions for:
  - TAM: Your Total Available Market (everyone you potentially help).
  - SAM: Your Serviceable Available Market (the portion of TAM you will target).
  - SOM: Your Share Of the Market (the portion of SAM that you project that you will realistically reach).

  Once you have identified your key market segments, include details of trends (such as are they growing or shrinking?) And highlight the market's evolving changes and requirements.

- **Your ideal customer profiles** – What are your customers' primary needs and wants?
- **Information on your competitors** – How are your competitors positioning themselves?
- **Positioning statement** – How do you plan on differentiating your business from the competition? For example:
  - Low-price solution or premium luxury brand?
  - What features or benefits do you offer that your competitors don't?
- **Market risks** – how do you intend to manage them? Where do you see your company in the landscape of other solutions?
- **Pricing of your products and services** – Once you know what your overall positioning strategy is, you can look at the pricing. Price sends a very strong message to consumers and can be an important tool to communicate your positioning. If you are offering a premium product, a premium price will quickly communicate that message. Some basic rules that you should follow:
  - **Covering your costs**. You should be charging your customers more than it costs you to deliver your product or service. However, there can be exceptions to this.
  - **Primary and secondary profit centre pricing**. Your initial price may not be your primary profit centre. For example, you may sell your product at, or below, cost and make your profit on a secondary product or service such as one that has a higher value or as a maintenance or support contract to go along with the purchase.
  - **Matching the market rate**. Your prices will need to match up with consumer demand and expectations. If the price is too high you may end up with no customers, but if you price too low people may undervalue your products and services and you could end up making no profit or even a loss, which would be unsustainable.
- **Three pricing strategies:**
  - **Cost-plus pricing**. You can look at your costs and then mark up your offering from there. This is usually called "cost-plus

pricing" and can be effective for manufacturers where covering initial costs is critical.

- o **Market-based pricing.** Look at the current landscape of competitors and then price based on what the market is expecting. You could price at the high end or low end of the market to establish your positioning.
- o **Value pricing.** The "value pricing" model is where you determine the price based on how much value you are providing to your customer.

4. Advertising and Promotional Strategies.

An advertising and promotion plan should include an overview of all the different kinds of advertising that you plan to communicate with your prospects and customers. It's important that you measure the costs of your promotional campaigns against the results that they achieve.

Here are a few tips that many business owners know about, but fail to use to their advantage:

- **Strategic alliances –** You may rely on working closely with another company in a form of partnership, which helps to provide access to a target market segment for your company while allowing your partner to offer a new product or service to their customers. If you have partnerships already established, it's important to detail these in your business plan.
- **Public relations** – Get the media to cover your company and products.
- **Content marketing** – Publish useful information, tips, and advice so that your target market can get to know your company. Content marketing is about teaching and educating your prospects on topics that they are interested in, not just on the features and benefits that you offer.
- **Social media** – For most businesses, it is essential to have a presence on the social media that your customers are on. Register for them all, test them and then concentrate on the ones that are working best for you.

5. Organisational Management

This section of your business plan is your chance to show off your key assets and your management team's superstar qualities, so make sure you highlight the key areas of expertise and qualifications for each member of the team. Anyone reading your plan and any potential investors will want to know that you have a competent team in place that can deliver. The chances of being successful are much higher if you have the right organisational management team and structure in place for your company.

Things to include:

- Key staff
- Premises
- Equipment
- Suppliers
- Operational risks

Financial plan

This is often what entrepreneurs find most daunting, Business financials for most start-ups are less complicated than you think, and a business degree is not required to build a solid forecast. That said, if you need additional help, there are plenty of tools and resources out there to help you. A typical financial plan will have monthly sales and revenue projections for the first 12 months, and then annual projections for three to five years.

The following are details of the financial statements that you should include in your business plan, and a brief overview of what should be in each section.

Sales Forecast

Your sales forecast is your projections of how much you are going to sell over the next few years, which is typically broken down into a row for each core product or service that you are offering.

Start-up costs

This is all the costs that you will incur in getting the business off the ground and ready to start trading.

Profit and Loss Forecast (P&L)

The profit and loss forecast is where your numbers all come together and show if the company is making a profit or loss.

A typical P&L will include the following:

- Sales (or income or revenue).
- Cost of goods sold (COGS).
- Gross margin.
- Operating expenses.
- Total operating expenses.
- Operating income.
- Interest, taxes, depreciation, and amortisation.
- Total expenses.
- Net profit.

Funding Requirements

When seeking or pitching for investment, it is important to have a clear and accurate picture of your requirements and how they will be returned to any investors and on what terms.

Things to include are:

- How much of your own capital have you invested in the business?
- What is the current valuation of the business?
- How much funding are you looking for?
- What will the funds be used for?
- What terms are you offering if you are pitching to investors?

Cash-flow Forecast

The cash-flow statement keeps track of how much cash you have available in the company bank account at any given point. It starts with the amount of cash you have on hand and adds new cash, which is received through cash sales and paid invoices, and then subtracts cash that you have paid out on bills, loans, taxes, etc.

Your cash-flow forecast will show you when you might be low on cash, and when it might be the best time to buy new equipment. Your cash-flow statement will help you figure out how much money you might need to raise or borrow to grow your company. An operating business must have cash available to pay the bills otherwise it will end up going out of business.

Balance Sheet

The balance sheet lists the assets, liabilities, and the owner's equity and provides an overview of the financial health of your business. The net worth of the company is calculated by deducting the company's liabilities from the company assets.

Managing Financial Risk

Your business plan should detail all the key assumptions that you have made. When you recognise your assumptions, you can set out to prove whether these are correct. The more that you can minimise your assumptions, the more likely it is that your business will succeed.

Exit Strategy

The last thing that you might be thinking about during your start-up is an exit strategy, but it is something that is important to consider right from the beginning. At some point in the future, you are highly likely to either want to get out of the business by selling it or passing it on to someone else. The last thing you want to do is have to close it down.

You don't need to go into a lot of detail, but you should identify some companies that might be interested in buying your business if you are successful.

Chapter 16 of this book goes into more detail on selling your business.

Business Start-Up Checklist

As many people aren't familiar with the steps to start a business, this checklist covers the key tasks and activities you need to know pre- and post-launch to hit the ground running:

Step 1: Business Name and Logo

A business name and logo are the first entry points and differentiators between you and your competitors. Your customers will instantly make judgements whether they want to part with their cash based on their initial appeal, which is why the name and logo are so important. We don't get a second chance to make a first impression, so the more appealing and memorable you can be the better.

Here are a list of some general dos and don'ts when it comes to selecting a name and logo for your company:

Do:

- Think about your products and services.
- Think about the values and mission of the business.
- Think about the market you are entering.
- Think about the people you are targeting.
- Make it easy to spell.
- Make it memorable.
- Make it as simple as possible.
- Make it easy to recognise.
- Pick a name that can grow with your business.
- Make it so that you like saying it, hearing it and seeing it.
- Ask friends and family for ideas.
- Create a shortlist.
- Test out your potential names to see what they think.

Don't

- Make it personal to you.
- Inject humour if it's not appropriate.
- Don't be boring.
- Make it area specific.

When you have a shortlist of proposed business names, you can carry out a check online at Companies House to find out if the name has already been registered by an existing company or not. You can't register a company with the same name as an existing company, so it is important to check as soon as possible. It is also important to check that your proposed business name is not the same as a registered trademark and you can also check the trademark register online.

Once you have decided on your business name and done the checks, it's time to register the company with HMRC (must) and at Companies House (if applicable) and open accounts on all social media channels and make sure you purchase the domain name – even if you don't plan to use them straight away.

Once you have the name registered, you can look to finalising the company logo. It is possible to have a nice company logo created by a graphics designer for a relatively low cost, and is money well spent to create a professional, appealing image. The more information that you can provide, the easier and quicker it will be for the designer to produce, which will help keep the cost down.

Keep your brand identity consistent with the same logo and strapline, so that your name and logo are instantly recognisable.

Step 2: Organise Communications

It is important to make sure that prospects and customers can easily find and communicate with you by telephone, email, website, social media networks and post.

Some of the issues to consider are:

- Are you going to trade from home and, if so, do you want to use your home address for business communication? There are companies who can provide you with a prestigious business trading address.
- Are you going to have a dedicated landline and mobile number for the business? It's good to separate them but it is also good to keep costs low, particularly in the early days.
- Respond promptly on social media networks.
- Ideally have a professional email address that matches the company and website domains. For example, Joe@joebloggs.com

Step 3: Get Support In Place

Make sure you have someone you can talk to regularly about your business. There will be great days and there will also be days when things go wrong and your motivation will slump.

The key areas to have support in are:

- Having a good coach or mentor who has walked the path that you are about to take and can support you along the journey. It is important to find one that you feel you connect with and can work with. Having a good coach / mentor can be the difference between success and failure. Many people feel that they cannot afford one, but the better question is: can you afford not to.
- Having a good accountant who can be worth their weight in gold.
- Being part of a mastermind of like-minded people who are on the same journey or further down the path.

Step 4: Register the Company with HMRC (Must) and Companies House (If Applicable)

If you have chosen to trade under a company structure, you can register the company yourself or employ a professional company to do it for you.

Step 5: Financing Your Business Start-up

It is important to give careful and serious thought to how you will finance your business. This includes start-up costs and expenses, as well as operational and running costs and personal income management. Some small businesses are self-funded, whilst others require external funding. If you are planning to self-fund your business, you might want to consider keeping your existing job while setting up and establishing your business to reduce the risks.

Some of the ways to finance a start-up business, include:

- Personal savings.
- Selling up some of your possessions that you can do without.
- Overdrafts.

- 0% credit cards.
- Borrowing from friends and family.
- Small business loans.
- Investors.
- Business angels.
- Government loans or grants.
- Crowd-funding.

There are advantages and disadvantages to each of these methods.

Step 6: Set Up A Business Bank Account

Having a business bank account is essential if you set up a company, as it is a separate legal entity to you. If you are a sole trader, it is recommended but not essential, but keeping very clear and separate accounts is a must.

Step 7: Tax and Accounting

Register with HMRC for certain taxes. This will depend on the legal structure that you choose. Some examples are Corporation Tax, VAT, PAYE and Self-Assessment. I would advise that you consult and appoint an accountant for assistance and guidance on running your business in a cost-effective and tax-efficient manner and concentrate on the fun and more joyous areas of starting and growing a business. You won't regret it – unless you're a glutton for punishment.

Step 8: Start Accounting For Everything

You can appoint an accountant or set up your own simple book-keeping system. An online accounting software package can save you a lot of time and effort, while keeping your records up to date and in order. If you plan to do the bookkeeping within the business and outsource the accounting, it is advisable to have the same accounting software as your accountants or ensure that the systems are compatible if different.

Step 9: Sort Out Insurance Cover

Insurance can protect you and your business against risks, including: accidents, sickness, theft and legal fees. The cover you need will depend on the nature of the business and how you run it. Chapter 14 goes into more detail on safeguarding your business.

Step 10: Get Compliant

Make sure that you satisfy all regulatory issues eg. health & safety, licensing, data protection. More on this in Chapter 14: Safeguarding Your Business.

Step 11: Keep Costs As Low As Possible

Until your business is established and sustainable revenue and profits are being generated, and cashflow is operating smoothly, it is important to keep as tight a rein on your expenditure as you possibly can.

Step 12: Manage Your Cash Flow

It is important that you personally understand cashflow. Once you have your cashflow forecast complete, it is important to keep it updated with actual figures on a regular basis. A simple spreadsheet is usually adequate for doing it yourself or you can have a bookkeeper / bookkeeping software system or accountant to keep it updated for you.

Step 13: Business Kit

Depending on which type of business you decide to start, you will need some office furniture and equipment and maybe some other plant, tools and equipment to produce and deliver your products and services. It is a good idea to be resourceful and keep costs to a minimum.

Step 14: Suppliers and Manufacturers

Depending on which type of business you go into, you are going to need a supply chain of suppliers and manufacturers. This is covered in more detail in Chapter 8.

Take time to check them out, get references and samples, etc. and if you are going to be dealing with overseas suppliers and manufacturers, it may be beneficial to register your business for VAT before placing any orders.

Businesses in certain countries are required to charge VAT to overseas customers that are not VAT registered. It is best to speak to an accountant and tax expert in your area of business on this as their advice could save you a great deal of money. You can also speak to your local government business agency for support and advice.

Step 15. Workspace / Business Premises

Running your new business start-up from home is a good way to keep costs down, especially in the early days when you're just starting out and not yet making much (if any) profit or positive cashflow. However, that's not always an option for everyone.

If you are working from home, there are some important things to consider:

- You can claim a percentage of household running costs as business expenses.
- If you rent the property where you live, check your lease to see that working from home is allowed.
- Check for possible Capital Gains Tax implications if you own your own home.
- Check if planning permission may be required. If you expect regular business visitors or to employ someone who'll be working from your home, ask your local authority planning department for advice.
- It is also important to have relevant insurance cover in place. More on safeguarding your business and self in Chapter 14.

If your business requires dedicated premises, you will need to consider the size of premises you require, how much you can afford to pay, which location will work best, whether you should lease, licence or purchase the premises, etc. Your local authority should be able to provide information about business premises and rates in your area.

Give yourself plenty of time to find somewhere appropriate. You could use an agent if you don't have the time and knowledge, to help you find the right premises for your needs and budget.

If you work online using a laptop most of the time, co-working spaces where you can hire a desk or room by the hour or hang out and work in the communal areas can be a great cost-effective way to work, whilst avoiding the isolation of working from home alone. It's also a great space to get support from other like-minded people and you never know what opportunities can come from working and networking in these places.

Step 16. Websites

Having a website is important in today's world. It is your virtual shopfront and should be appealing and easy to navigate and for the customer to get good information and content. The complexity of the functions of the website will depend on the nature of the business that you intend to operate. A good way to get ideas and take inspiration is by checking out competitors' websites, or websites that you visit and find appealing and easy to use. Some of the things to look out for are:

- Visually pleasing.
- Easy to use.
- Responsive.
- Informative.

You can build a website yourself now through several online sites, which provide standard or professional templates that you can personalise and adapt to meet your needs. Alternatively, you can get a professional web designer to build a website for you.

Step 17. Social Media

Social media is an important consideration. It is one of the most effective and affordable ways to connect with your target market to promote your business. Figure out which ones work best for you, and concentrate on posting relevant and interesting content on a regular basis to engage with customers and to build trust, confidence and relationships.

Step 18. Licences and Permits

Depending on the type of business you are setting up, you may require licences and/or permits in order to trade. Your local authority should be able to help you or point you in the right direction to ensure that you have the relevant licenses and permits in place to trade legally.

Step 19. Data Protection and Information Rights

If you will be holding information on any individuals, including customers, employees or suppliers, the Data Protection Act requires you to protect that information.

Step 20. Intellectual Property (IP) Protection

Intellectual Property relates to trademarks, patents, copyright and design rights. You can protect an idea, product designs, work of art, company logo, etc., to prevent others from using it, stealing it, copying it or selling it without your permission.

Step 21. Money Laundering Regulations

Some types of businesses are legally required to comply with Money Laundering Regulations, which involves carrying out due diligence measures on all customers to ensure they are who they say they are.

Step 22. Product Labelling and Packaging

Not all goods require labels but if they do, the way they are packaged and presented can make a lasting impression and add value to your products, particularly if you are selling luxury items.

If your products require labelling, it is important that all information is accurate. It is a criminal offence to include any misleading information on product labels.

Some sectors such as selling food and drink, children's products, furniture, footwear, etc., have special rules that must be followed. Safety information must be included on any products that are dangerous.

For specific advice on labelling and packaging requirements, it is best to contact your local Trading Standards Office to ensure that you are trading within the law.

Step 23. Product Delivery and Returns

If you will be sending out goods by post, it is important to have a secure and reliable delivery service in place. The type of service may depend on the volume of orders. If it is large quantities you might have to use a courier, or if you are only delivering on an occasional basis, you may be better using Royal Mail and Parcel Force.

Some other considerations to make are:

- How much will you charge?
- What delivery options will you offer?
- Will you provide international delivery?

You can look at your competitors' delivery policies and fees for ideas and guidance and then match or exceed their services.

With regards customer returns, there are certain legal obligations:

- You must offer a refund if a product is faulty, not as described, or does not do what it is supposed to do.
- Customers are entitled to a full return if a product is returned within 14 days. Many businesses increase the return period to 30 days.
- You will also need to think about whether you offer free returns. In certain situations, businesses must pay the return postage fees. For example, when goods are faulty.
- Offering free returns can be beneficial and have a positive impact by encouraging sales. Anything that you can do to remove a barrier for the customer is good for business.

Step 24. Business Stationery

Business stationery should be customised in a consistent format with your business name, company logo and contact details. All companies are legally required to state their name, registration number and registered office details on all the various forms of stationery.

The types of stationery you may require and wish to use include:

- Letterheads.
- Compliment slips.
- Business cards.
- Invoices.
- Purchase orders.
- Receipts.
- Returns slips and labels.
- Brochures.
- Leaflets and flyers.
- Discount and gift vouchers.
- Printed envelopes and labels.

Stationery can be an effective way to establish a strong brand and promote your business.

Use environmentally-friendly products wherever possible.

Step 25. Marketing Plan

Start marketing as early as possible in a targeted manner. You must introduce yourself to the world and let your potential customers know you exist. Always be experimenting, testing and reviewing which marketing methods are working for you. Test small and keep scaling what works until you reach the numbers that you need.

Step 26. Employing Staff

Many entrepreneurs launch a start-up with the mindset that they can do everything themselves, but this doesn't have to be the case and can be a block on the growth and success of the business. Learning to delegate is a vital skill to develop early on and is key to growing a business.

Recruiting staff can be a big step for any start-up and for a small business. I remember taking on my first employees and it was nerve-racking, but if the business can afford to do it, I would encourage people to go for it. Before employing someone directly within the company though, it is worth investigating if the service that you are looking for can be outsourced to a freelance individual. There are advantages and disadvantages to this, but it can be a good way of maintaining flexibility while you grow until there is certainty that you can provide an ongoing full or part-time position.

Building a team of great people with uniquely-different skills and knowledge will accelerate growth and for a business that is just getting off the ground with little money, strategy or even product in place, having the right people is essential.

When hiring, hire like-minded people who share your passion and drive and make sure their skillset complements yours.

When you employ people, you will have certain legal, and health and safety, obligations and responsibilities to comply with such as:

- Registering with HMRC as an employer.
- Operating payroll.
- Having Employer's Liability Insurance.
- Adhering to Health and Safety Regulations.
- Having an eligible workplace pension scheme that you can enrol employees in to.

Step 27: Keep Or Quit The Day Job

One of the common misconceptions about starting up a business is that you must quit your job to have the time and energy to dedicate to building it. This depends on the nature of your start-up and is not always true. If we look back to the example that I shared earlier in the book, where I had built up enough business through working in my spare time that would keep me busy for several months and give me an income whilst I acquired more work, it meant that I had a jumpstart and massively reduced the risk. There are some famous entrepreneurs who kept their jobs until their start-ups evolved to the stage where they had become safer bets and then went on to become very successful.

Examples include:

- **Phil Knight:** worked two jobs for six years. Working for Price Waterhouse by day and an entrepreneur building Nike by night that has become a $30 billion company.
- **Steve Wozniak:** worked for Hewlett-Packard even a year after inventing the Apple computer.
- **Sara Blakely:** sold fax machines door-to-door for seven years before making it big with her pantyhose innovation. She was rejected by every manufacturing company she took her idea to. In the end her perseverance paid off, and made her the youngest self-made billionaire in America.

To make the transition between your full-time job and your dream business, you just have to be a little creative.

Here are five creative approaches that successful entrepreneurs have used:

- Hustle in the evenings and weekends.
- Work part-time.
- Ask your boss if you can work flexible or fewer hours.
- Take a sabbatical.
- Partner with your employer

Management researchers, Joseph Raffiee and Jie Feng, tracked a group of 5,000 would-be entrepreneurs in America from 1994 to 2008, and looked at who became entrepreneurs during the 15-year period in question. The participants in the study were in their 20s, 30s, 40s, and 50s, and they started a wide variety of businesses. The results showed that regardless of industry, those who kept their day jobs were 33 percent less likely to fail in their new venture.

Many people believe that starting a business is risky, and it is, but the risk can be greatly reduced if the right research and steps are taken. The same people fail to consider that working for an employer and relying on them for an income to support your family for the rest of their life can be the greatest risk of all. We hear that a large percentage of businesses fail, and we are seeing more and more big-name well-established businesses disappearing now with the speed of change in the market place. If you are currently an employee who is considering starting your own business but not quite sure due to the risks involved, it is worth considering that you might be working for a company that will disappear.

Keeping your job in the beginning whilst building your business on the side is one way of mitigating some of the risks and alleviating some of the pressure that people put themselves under to be successful.

Step 28: Make Sure You Can Walk Before You Run!

It is important to set up your business in a logical order and leave room for growth as you become more knowledgeable and successful. Many new businesses fail because they try to run too fast in the beginning and either run out of cash or because they make too big a move too quickly which leads to a mistake that takes them out of the game. Succeeding is all about stacking the odds in your favour, which comes from a combination of knowledge, experience, support, plus dedication, persistence and consistency and having a well-balanced life.

It is important to stay focused and look at the long game. Most people overestimate what they can achieve in one year and underestimate what they can achieve in five years.

CHAPTER 7

STRATEGIES

Business strategies have changed dramatically in the past two decades.

Many of the big names and brands that were around a couple of decades ago no longer exist. Some examples include:

- Woolworths
- Blockbuster
- Kodak
- MFI
- Toys R Us

Most of the largest companies that exist today were not even started two (or even one) decades ago. Some examples include:

- Google
- Amazon
- Facebook
- Uber
- Airbnb
- Netflix

Most businesses do not go out of business due to competition; they go out of business due to failing to adapt their strategy to meet customers' expectations. Some examples include:

- Amazon didn't kill retailers, poor customer service did.
- Apple didn't kill the music industry, being forced to buy full-length albums did.
- Uber didn't kill the taxi business, limited access and fare control did.
- Netflix didn't kill blockbusters; late payment fees did.
- Airbnb didn't kill the hotel industry, limited availability and price options did.

Many of the world's most successful and largest business brands today are connectors. For example:

- Google provides an online search engine that connects people with information but produces no content.
- Facebook provides an online platform that connects people with people.
- Amazon provides an online platform connects customers with products but produces few of its own products.
- Airbnb provides an online platform that connects people who have a spare room with people who require a room, but the company owns none of their own rental properties.
- Uber provides an online platform that connects car owner/drivers with people who need a taxi, but the company owns none of their own cars.

Some of the top brands that were developed more than two decades ago that still exist today are:

- Apple
- Microsoft
- McDonald's
- Burger King
- Toyota

In the past, we have seen success stories from the likes of Andrew Carnegie and the steel industry, the Rockefellers and the oil industry, Henry Ford and the car industry. Today, we see companies such as Google, Facebook, Amazon, Microsoft, Apple and the like being the huge success stories.

Today's Most Successful Business Strategies

Times are changing so fast, particularly in the world of business. How businesses interact with their customers, how companies innovate, and even the very business models that organisations are built on are all undergoing rapid change.

Yet, from what I've seen, many businesses are failing to keep up, and far too many are operating on outdated business models.

If you're leading a company, whether it's small or large, a brand-new start-up or an established business, you'll need to understand the latest business models and assess how they might apply to your company. That's why I've picked some of the most successful business models for 2019 and beyond, to take a look at.

The Subscription-Based Business

Instead of selling a product or a service as a one-off, some companies operate a subscription or ongoing service model, building a more intimate understanding of their customers in the process. For example, if we compare Netflix and Disney:

- Disney produces a film, releases it in cinemas, and the film is either a hit or it's not. They won't necessarily understand exactly how many people watched it and how much those viewers liked it.
- Netflix, on the other hand, has an intensely close customer relationship. They understand and have valuable data on exactly how many users have streamed a movie or series, whether they gave up part-way through and watched something else, whether they then went on to watch more content starring the same actor, etc.

Another example is Dollar Shave Club (grooming subscription company) versus Gillette (razor manufacturer with limited direct customer relationship). The Dollar Shave Club has access to valuable customer data that Gillette does not have with its business model.

The Platform-Based Business

This model is closely linked to the sharing economy and subscription models. Platforms are particularly powerful when they are combined with a subscription model. Well-known examples of platform businesses include Facebook, Uber and Airbnb. Platforms provide an online or physical platform for parties to interact with each other and deliver value for users by facilitating direct connections and exchanges between people. The more valuable the platform is to the user, the more successful the business becomes. In return, the business gets a detailed insight into its users.

The Social, Authentic Business

Today's authentic businesses share their opinions and stand up for their values. Typically, the CEO is active on social media and employees are actively encouraged to be brand ambassadors. Crucially, the brand itself has a lively and engaging social media presence, with a strong brand message that really connects with the target audience.

The Employee-Centric Business

The way we work is changing and the way companies now must go about attracting people is changing. Companies still need great people, so it is vital that companies adapt and become employee-centric. This means offering people an attractive place to work, flexibility, space to grow and the means to develop their career. Google is a prime example of an employee-centric business today.

The Partner-Centric Business

Companies are increasingly becoming more partner-centric, where they outsource specific areas of business by tapping into on-demand services from other specialist business service providers. They create attractive networks of partnerships and are a valuable partner to others.

A typical small or mid-sized business might outsource their social media strategy to one business, their IT support to another, website design to another company and so on.

In today's rapidly-changing business world, some larger companies still have a lot to learn from this flexible, scalable model.

The Customer Value-Obsessed Business

This model applies to every business as business is all about solving customers' problems, anticipating their needs, making their lives easier and removing any friction or hassle. Amazon is an obvious and great example of this.

You can't mention Amazon and strategy together and not think about personalisation. Their 'recommendations' tool has revolutionised the way retailers think about their customers, and importantly, the data they create. It kicked off a trend that has seen retailers, use data to give their customers what they want, when they want it.

The Constant-Innovation Business

The ability to constantly innovate is crucial and has never been more important to the ongoing success of a business. Some of the most successful businesses in the world are constantly innovating and transforming, even if it means cannibalising their own products and services to create something new. For example: Apple's iPod was effectively killed off quickly by the launch of their iPhone.

Today, we see Apple and Samsung innovating their smartphones with a new model of their flagship iPhone and Galaxy ranges launched every year.

The Data-Driven Business

Companies recognise that data is one of their critical business assets today. The data-driven business has measures in place to understand exactly what's happening now, and uses that information to make better decisions, refine operations, and even create new revenue streams. Companies who value data are the ones in pole position to experiment and innovate at a faster pace.

The Tech-Based Business

We are living in a time of rapid technological innovation and change. A.I., big data, blockchain, 3D printing, virtual reality are just some of the massive changes that are taking place right now.

Many of the most successful companies on the planet today are tech businesses: Apple, Google, Microsoft, Amazon and Facebook to name a few. Regardless of your sector and company size, it's vital your organisation embraces technology. If you don't, you risk being left behind.

Many of today's most successful businesses have managed to combine a number, if not all, of these business models to catapult their companies to success. Some examples are:

- Amazon and their Amazon Prime annual subscription and monthly music subscription models.
- Microsoft and their Office 365 monthly subscription model.
- Facebook generates massive revenue from members advertising to other Facebook users.
- Google has Google Play monthly subscription and monthly subscription for use of their G-Suite, which competes with Microsoft's Office 365 package.

The relationship that an organisation holds with its customer has changed significantly.

Today, building a global brand requires a lot more than translating your website into different languages. The most successful companies understand that consistent and universally-appealing products must be combined with an understanding of local culture and tastes in terms of service. Let's look at Apple as an example.

- Apple is seen as one of *the* most famous and successful global brands of our time, so it's a good example to look at and learn a thing or two from. Success leaves clues as they say. So, what can we learn from Apple?
- When it comes to its products, the company has opted for a one-size-fits-all strategy, with their product designs the same regardless of region or country. Whilst this can be a dangerous strategy, Apple's minimalist and intuitive approach has resulted in products that have universal global appeal.
- However, Apple also understands where the transition between standardisation needs to end, and localisation needs to begin. The customer service protocol for each of its worldwide stores is tailored to suit local tastes and, despite having the same look and feel regardless of location, the content on the Apple site is carefully translated and localised for international audiences.
- Their pricing strategy has never been about cutting costs, they position themselves as a premium brand whose strategy has been to differentiate by quality. Coupled with relentless lifestyle marketing campaigns and a consistent brand image, they have been able to create

a 'halo effect' where customers continually crave the latest Apple product as if it were an addictive substance.

- Apple have also ramped up their supply chain strategies significantly over the last decade. Where previously on a new iPhone release day customers were unlikely to leave the store with their new iPhone in hand, now, the chances are a lot higher. Slick supply chains have always been an important focus and passion for CEO, Tim Cook, and he will be delighted that Apple's supply chain strategy is now getting their products to stores much quicker than before.

First Mover vs Early Adopter Strategy

One of the most common and big misconceptions in the business start-up world is that it's the idea that matters the most. The truth is, the world's most successful companies were rarely the first ones to innovate. First mover advantage is often a disadvantage – and a well-executed follower or early adopter strategy is highly likely to outperform a less well-executed 'first mover' strategy every single time. Here are some of the reasons why this happens:

- The market isn't well defined with first movers.
- The market doesn't even know your product exists and needs to be educated on its value.
- The technology will hold you back rather than power you to success.
- Every single person who comes after you will have the advantage of learning from your mistakes.

It's important to think very seriously about whether 'first mover' or 'smart follower / early adopter' are part of the best business strategies for you.

The diagram below shows a typical market sector or product lifecycle.

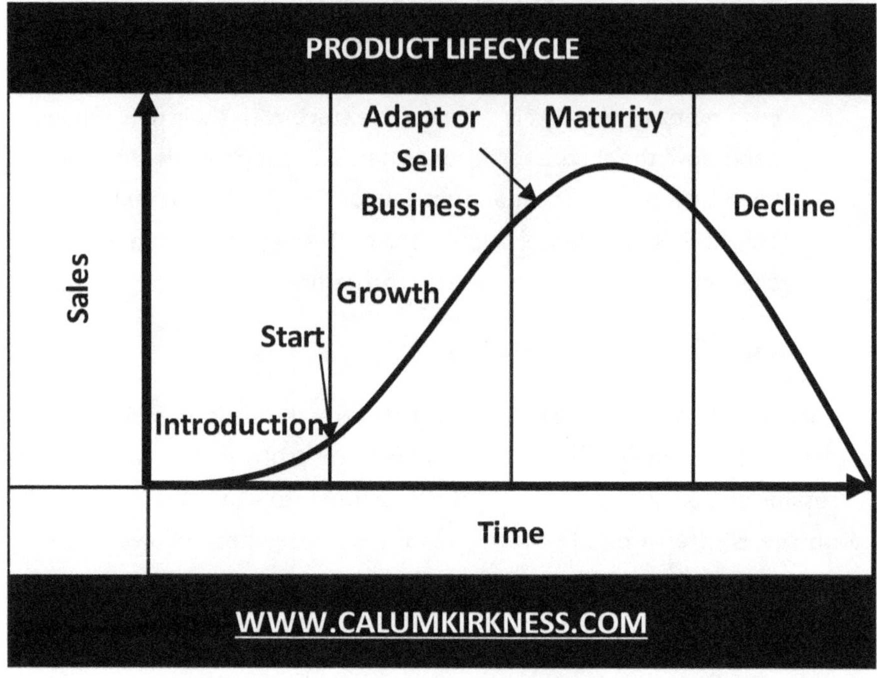

CHAPTER 8

SUPPLY CHAIN

Creating a successful business requires building and having a strong supply chain to support it. A supply chain is made up of all external people and organisations that you will engage with in order to run your business. A supply chain is usually made up of:

- Suppliers
- Strategic partners
- Specialist service providers
- Contractors

Building a supply chain takes time and effort and should be an ongoing process of improvement.

Your supply chain will only be as strong as the weakest link, hence why it is so important to develop a robust selection process.

As you will be regularly working with your supply chain, they should also be a good match with your values, strategies and systems.

When I am building my supply chains or when I am considering additions or replacements, I have developed some strategies to help me which are based on models that have been tried, tested and proven to be effective. For example, when I am making supply-chain decisions, I think about how a successful football club has been built up and how they succeed with certain managers and under-perform with others. I put myself in the position of the CEO and ask myself: what they would do and how would they approach building up the key people in the club, in order that it becomes or remains the most successful?

The CEO of a football club wouldn't employ a rugby coach to manage the club, and a football manager wouldn't sign up a few new rugby players to play in the team. You get my point: your supply chain members need to be experts in your chosen strategy and systems.

Your supply chain members may include:

- Legal advisor who is specialised in your area of business.
- Finance specialist in your area of business.
- Taxation specialist in your area of business.
- Specialist consultants.
- Specialist suppliers.
- Specialist contractors.
- Business partnerships.
- Investors.

How to find members for your supply chain:

- Google search.
- LinkedIn.
- Facebook.
- Business networking events.
- General networking events.
- Business functions.
- Social activities/hobbies.
- Advertisements.
- Private membership clubs.
- Recommendations/word of mouth.
- Always be alert and looking out, or listening for people/companies being talked about or recommended. Opportunities to build and strengthen your supply chain are everywhere!
- Always carry business cards with you.

5 Key Things To Look For In Your Supply Chain

Your supply chain members should be engaged to do the things that:

- You can't do.
- You don't enjoy doing.
- They can do better than you.
- They can do quicker than you.
- Are cheaper to do than the amount you can make by applying your time and expertise on other tasks.

7 Cs for building a winning team and supply chain:

    i.   Coaching
   ii.   Character
  iii.   Communication
  iv.   Commitment
   v.   Contagious energy
  vi.   Caring
 vii.   Consistency

It is a good idea to review your supply chain regularly.

Building a strong and reliable supply chain takes time, but once you have it in place it makes your life as a business owner much more efficient, more enjoyable and so much easier.

Joint Venture Partners As Part Of Your Supply Chain

Joint venture partners can also be considered as an important part of a supply chain.

There are four crucial elements to a successful joint venture partnership:

- A person or persons with the investment **funds**.
- A person or persons with the relevant **knowledge**.
- A person or persons with the relevant **experience**.
- A person or persons with the **time**.

It is very rare to find someone who has all four of the key components. When you can bring such people together, you can achieve much more than the individual parts and achieve a win-win outcome for all partners.

It is important that the JV partners bring a balance of the above to the venture and that it is strong enough in all areas to maximise the chances of success.

The sum of the JV should be greater than the individual parts, otherwise you are better outsourcing the areas where you require support.

Always consider:

- What value can you bring to the partnership?
- What would you like to get out of the partnership?
- Do you feel that all the other partners will benefit from the partnership?
- Can you work with all the partners in the joint venture?

Key Elements To Establish In Any Joint Venture Partnership:

- Number of parties.
- Purpose of the JV.
- Contribution of each party.
- Structure.
- Valuation/split.
- Management/control.
- Talent and resources.
- Contractual arrangements.
- Exit strategy and provisions.

Each of your service providers in your power team/JV partnerships should be performing at a high level of 80% out of 100%, or above, or you should be actively looking to replace them. It is also important to work with more than one service provider for each category if you can. A football club with no substitute goalkeeper would be putting themselves at high risk of losing a game, whereas a football team that had no substitute for their star striker might not be at such a great risk of losing games, but they would have a reduced chance of winning. This way, if one service provider lets you down, you are not left in a weak position. It also stimulates healthy competition to ensure competitive service between the supply chain members.

Some of the supply chain members will have little interaction with others and therefore it is not so important that they are a good fit with the other members of the team. Depending on how you structure your business, there may be some members of the supply chain who will be required to work often, and interact closely, with others. You want to encourage your supply chain to feel free to be creative and interact with other team members, so that you do not have to be relied upon all the time for decisions. Be clear on the level of decision making you want to be included in and, as time goes on, your team and supply chain will begin to form relationships which everyone will understand. Create documented standards and systemise all common procedures, which we will look at in greater detail later in the book.

When you are building your supply chain:

- Initially look for several suppliers – say, nine in each area of your supply chain.
- Select and interview six.
- Add a minimum of two, or ideally three, of the best in each section if they are suitable and meet your criteria.
- Always aim to have minimum of two suppliers, and ideally three, in all or as many areas of your business as possible.

Replace any members who are consistently underperforming without delay, and always be looking to strengthen your supply chain.

8 Cs for assessing and building your supply chain:

- **Competency** – Choose people who are experts in the service that you are looking for.
- **Commitment** – Work with people who are committed to providing a high level of service; if not, look to replace them.
- **Collaboration** – Your suppliers should be willing to collaborate with the team when required.
- **Culture** – Create a positive environment where team members can flourish.
- **Communication** – Make sure all communication is clear and avoids assumptions.
- **Creative** – Encourage creativity from the whole team.
- **Clarity** – Ensure that everyone is clear on the end goal and what is required from them.

- **Consequences** – Let the team members know that you are unable to accept poor performance, and this will lead to replacements being sought and appointed.

"Do what you do best and delegate the rest."
– Calum Kirkness

CHAPTER 9

SYSTEMS

"System-building is business building."
– Calum Kirkness

Without having good systems and processes in place in your business, it is impossible to build a business that runs smoothly in a consistent and predictable way that can be scaled. Having good systems and processes in place allows the business to operate on its own and scale to the next level without robbing you of all your time and freedom.

"Systems should run your business and
people should run your systems."
– Calum Kirkness

One of the biggest mistakes that I made throughout my earlier entrepreneurial journey was not understanding the importance of systems and processes and their value, and then investing time and effort to develop and implement them to free up my time. I was trapped in a vicious cycle of being too busy to have time to develop systems. If you don't take time to develop and implement them, you will never have time for yourself later and remain trapped in a vicious cycle.

For most business owners, there is a big difference between how they expected running their own business would be and the reality of how it is for them. Most business owners start their journey with the dream of having success that will bring them financial abundance and time freedom to enjoy life in a way that their previous jobs did not, which is a good dream and goal to have and is open and possible to everyone.

It is an unfortunate truth that most small business owners experience the opposite of what they set out to achieve and find themselves working harder than ever and worry about the business and their personal finances.

Why Does This Happen To So Many Entrepreneurs?

The problem is that most entrepreneurs are focusing on the wrong things, which means they are fundamentally off track about what it takes to run and build a successful business. We are all surrounded with so much information and distractions today – much of this is totally useless and has our focus constantly jumping around from one thing to the next. We also hear of things like multiple streams of income and new entrepreneurs make the mistake of trying to juggle too many things at the same time, boasting about working 16 or even 20 hours per day but achieving very little other than burning themselves out.

Having clear goals, focusing on them and building systems and processes to run your business, that other people run for you, is the key to building a successful business that you can work on rather than work in.

When you can build good systems and processes, it allows you to replicate yourself many times over. This is what allows your business to be scaled whilst freeing up your time and freedom, as well as giving you the financial freedom to enjoy your time and do the things that you would like to do.

Small business owners will never achieve their vision of freedom, financial abundance or fulfilment by making or answering more phone calls, dealing with customers and employees, or working longer hours. Going down that road is a sure path to disaster.

So, if working harder in your business is not the answer, what is? It is having systems and processes. Systems should run your business and people should run your systems or, better still, your systems can be automated using technology.

What Are The Benefits Of Systems?

Systems Are Predictable.

Imagine you operate a bakery business without having any systems in place for the baking of the cakes or how they are presented to the customer. Every day, the cakes would most likely come out and taste and look different. Some days they might be great – with the perfect combination of ingredients, the right amount of time in the oven and be out on display at the right time ready for the customer to see and be unable to resist. On other days, the wrong combination of ingredients might be used, they might not be mixed properly, they may be baked at the wrong temperature for the wrong amount of time and not be ready in the morning for the customer when they are looking for or expect them. They will also depend on which staff are on duty. It would be impossible to build a brand around your bakery without having systems in place. When a customer knows exactly what they are getting every time, they will remain loyal and travel far and wide to buy your products and services and spread the message far and wide. Word of mouth is still a very valuable means of marketing.

The same is true in every area of your business. If you follow up with a new lead differently every time, the experience you're delivering is going to be hit or miss. Some clients will view you as prompt and professional, while others might feel that you're dropping the ball and can't be trusted with their business.

To have consistency in the products or services you deliver, there must be a consistent and predictable way you do it every time. Many small business owners build these consistent systems naturally out of habit, but they don't clarify or document it, which means they cannot be scaled or become at risk if a key employee leaves.

When your systems are well documented and implemented, they become consistent and predictable, which allows you to make smarter, more confident decisions and moves.

Systems Are Delegatable

Until you have clear systems and processes in place, you are limited to one of three things:

1. Doing the work yourself.
2. Being frustrated with the employees who don't know how to do the work correctly.
3. Being hostage to an employee who does do the work correctly.

With clear systems, you can train someone who has the skills required for the job and provide clear expectations. The work will be accomplished the way you want it, every time. And if that great employee who does the work correctly leaves, you can simply train a new employee.

Systems Are Measurable

When things are done the same way each time, they become measurable.

Creating detailed systems works for every type of business without fail. If we go back to the bakery business example, if the recipe has a high level of detail, and the baker has the required skills or experience, you could expect them to make the cakes the same every time. You would also know how many cakes a baker can make in a day, how many customers come in to the shop on a typical day, and how many cakes you sell on average each day and week. Even if the cakes are the same each day, you might notice differences in sales depending on who is serving the customers. Even things like having the right temperature and smell in the shop will affect results.

If we look at another example, let's assume your sales reps all have different sales presentations. Some salespeople will get dramatically better results than others, but you won't know why or how. If there was a documented sales presentation in place and new sales team members are trained on it, you can expect to achieve more consistent results that are close to others who have gone before them and expect a similar number of calls each day, week, month, which all helps predict the number of leads, sales, results.

You can also look to the qualities of the salesperson who is achieving the best results and look to include these in the systems for others to follow.

Systems Are Improvable

When the details of all areas of your business are measured, you can get a clear picture of what is working and what is not and take measures to make improvements on a regular basis.

You might know that your current sales presentation on average inspires 25% of the prospects who hear it to buy your main product. Armed with this knowledge, you could try a new style of presentation, share the benefits in a new way, shorten it or make it longer as necessary. Soon, you'd be able to measure your new results and determine whether the changes you made were an improvement over the previous presentation. From there, you could try again and experiment your way to a more effective presentation. Or a better cake, better packaging, customer service or advertising. This can be applied to all parts of your business. With systems in place, you can create a measurably better business over time by using the one strategy that is time-tested and proven to work in all businesses, which is trial and error.

Systems Are Scalable

Systems and processes are what lay the foundation for your businesses to become scalable. Once they are in place and have been tried and tested and achieving the desired results with a high degree of predictability, scaling becomes a simple matter of adding resources and also means that they can be automated.

If you want to bake more cakes, then you need to order more ingredients, employ more bakers and increase the number of servers in the shop. Depending on the scale, you might need to increase the size of the premises also. Likewise, if you want to increase your sales, hire another salesperson and train them based on the systems.

Systems Are Automatable

When companies embrace automation, it takes scalability to a whole new level in a business. Most systems and processes that are repetitive can be automated, and the biggest benefit of automation is that it is more reliable than humans in making sure the task is completed in the same way every time. Of course, not every system is automatable, but for those that are, employing software and machines to reliably, instantly and efficiently operate things can be a complete game-changer.

When McDonald's developed processes for their fast food operations back in the 1940s they automated their entire internal processes so that the employees could focus their time and attention on the customers. This led to increased productivity, improved customer service and satisfaction and scalability on a global scale. The good news is automation isn't just for huge corporations and tech giants.

It is becoming increasingly easier for companies to automate systems in every industry now, by replacing high-cost systems managed by people with low-cost, high-volume systems managed by software and machines.

It is important to keep in mind that a process should not be automated without thoroughly testing it first to ensure it works. If possible, once the ideal process has been mapped out, developed and tested, it is then time to implement it. Once implemented, it is important to keep track of the statistics needed to measure the effectiveness of your processes over time and continue making improvements.

Many employees fear the process of automation believing that it will do them out of a job. It is important to educate your employees on the benefits of automation – this will create more freedom for them to focus on tasks that require creativity and human intelligence. They can leave the hard work to the software and machines and focus on the bigger picture, working towards moving the business forward.

Systems Are Valuable And Sellable

Having good systems and processes in place is a game changer that can add significant value to your business in the eyes of prospective buyers and/or investors.

All prospective buyers and/or investors want to know that a business will remain viable even if the business owner, or some of the key members of staff, leave the company completely. It is a fact of life that people who work in a business won't always stay with the company, but systems and processes will. This means prospective buyers want to see that there are easy-to-follow, detailed systems and processes in place that they can use to train new people and continue running the business. System-building is at the heart of building a business that frees up your time and creates value that is saleable.

Business owners are not alone in their struggle to manage all the moving parts in a business.

The transition to greater automation can come with its challenges, particularly during the early period, but once they are in place the results can transform a business.

Where To Begin Systemising

Most entrepreneurs agree with the idea of systemisation but feel overwhelmed at the prospect of actually making it happen, often believing they don't have the time or that it will cost too much to put in place or they may even feel scared of systems being copied and replicated by an employee who later leaves. That is a scarcity mindset that you cannot afford to have if you wish to be successful.

Here are five steps to get started:

Step 1 – List all the responsibilities for every position in the business.

At first, it can be difficult for employees to identify exactly what they do all day and break it down into detailed chunk-size pieces.

An effective method is to have them write down everything they do all day, every day, for a one week, two weeks or even a full month. Once they have a complete list of their responsibilities they can be thoroughly documented, systemised and included in the operations manual.

Step 2 – Get the employees to write the detailed processes involved with those responsibilities.

Getting the employees to write the detailed processes involved with their responsibilities can have great benefits over someone else writing them and then imposing them on the employee. The employee feels valued and empowered to contribute to developing a system that works and is efficient and in their best interests. This doesn't mean leaving them without support, which is important to have in place to help them, particularly if the process is completely new to them.

Step 3 – Document processes in order of urgency.

The first priority is to get any employee who may leave their role soon – due to promotion, moving to another company, or even going on vacation – to document the processes they go through within their current role, first. This makes it much easier for their new replacement to quickly pick up where they left off and for the transition for everyone to be much smoother. A system should detail each step so thoroughly that any qualified person can complete the job simply by following it. Even the process of writing down all the steps can help employees identify where their inefficiencies are, so that plans and steps can be taken to correct and improve them.

Step 4 – Store the processes on a shared knowledge base where others can access them.

It is important to have the operations manual for the business stored in an easy-to-find communal location where anyone can look up the systems and processes. It could be online in a shared drive or in hard copy in the office location where they are based, or ideally both. This means no distracting messages to managers asking for guidance or time wasted as an employee aimlessly searches for instructions.

While writing systems can be a time-consuming process, it is important to remember that they'll ultimately reduce the time it takes to complete tasks. By getting this work done, you're creating the opportunity to delegate or even automate these responsibilities and building a path to create a scalable business that is much easier to manage.

Step 5 – Improve and make changes as necessary.

It is important to regularly review the company systems and processes and continually look for areas and ways to improve. As the employees continue to test and practise the processes, they may find inefficiencies that can be improved or removed completely. The rate of change and improvement may be rapid in the early days and then slow down. It is a good idea to hold weekly or monthly meetings in the beginning, which can then be extended to quarterly, bi-annually or annually once the systems and processes have become well refined. Over time, you can even create a process for reviewing, assessing, and improving different internal business processes.

When To Improve Your Systems

In the early days of developing and implementing systems and processes in your business, things may not always work out as well as intended and this is the time when persistence is important.

In most small businesses, when things go wrong and a customer does not get the experience that they expected, systems and processes aren't such a big deal. You can usually apologise, make it right, and fix your process. But if you want to scale the business and have a business that you work on rather than in, it is crucial that you have systems in place to handle 99% of the business processes.

Here Are 4 Main Reasons It's Time To Update And Improve Your Systems:

1. There is a glitch in the system that leads to a breakdown in the processes

This can either be the result of the process not working or the employee failing to follow the process. It is important to establish the reason and get to the root of the problem before taking steps to change and improve the system.

When the process has been followed and things still didn't go well, it is time to take a careful look at how the processes can be improved to avoid any repeat occurrences and then implement the steps required.

When it comes down to human error and not following the process, there is no point in changing the process. It is better to educate and train the employee on the importance of the process and why they need to follow it.

2. There are changes in how the business or processes operate

Whenever there is a significant change in the business, it will normally have some effect on the systems and processes and things will need to be updated to reflect the new changes.

Once the new changes are developed and introduced, it is important to communicate the changes throughout the organisation to ensure people are handling the flow efficiently and not doing double work. Seeing double work being undertaken is one of my major dislikes, which can lead to a lot of problems in the workplace such as confusion, friction, frustration and reduced morale.

Other changes that can lead to a review being required are the introduction of new laws, changes to existing laws or industry rules, the introduction of new technology in the business, etc.

3. New ideas are introduced

Entrepreneurs are always looking for new and better ways to do something and these ideas can come at any time, anywhere. Sometimes you'll get a new idea from reading an article, seeing how another business operates or getting a tip from an employee or someone you know. It is a good idea to encourage employees to come up with new ideas that can lead to improvements and reward them if the idea is later launched in the business.

It is always best to test any ideas first before fully updating and implementing them in to the company's processes. Some ideas will work better than others. When they do lead to improvements, that's the time to update your system documentation to reflect what the organisation has learned.

4. Scheduled deep dives and desire to find efficiencies

During periods when the company is busy, there can be a tendency for ad hoc adjustments to be made to the company's systems and processes to address the immediate requirements and before you know it, the systems and processes have become overcomplicated and confusing. Hence the reason it is important to take the time to step back and reflect on what has been happening over the period since the last review. Involve everyone in the review process and get their feedback on things that haven't been working, leading to employee frustration or a drop in customer satisfaction.

While carrying out a deep-dive review into your company's processes, it is important to always be looking for opportunities to improve, simplify and streamline things.

Conducting a deep-dive review at least once a year is a good way to keep your business's improvements on track. In the early stages of developing systems and processes in a business, it is advisable to hold these review meetings monthly or quarterly.

By taking the time to step back and look at the bigger picture, you can save a lot of money and improve your customers' experiences.

The more you can successfully systemise the processes and then automate them, the easier it will be for you and your team to focus on creating new and/or greater value for your customers. Remember the greater the value you provide, the greater the reward.

Story About Starbucks and Systems

Here is a story that I once heard about the former CEO of Starbucks, Howard Schultz. When he was on a trip, he went in to visit one of the 29,000 Starbucks outlets as a regular customer and noticed that one of the lights was out in the outlet, which was not a good look.

There were several options available to Howard Schultz:

A. He could have spoken to the staff and asked them to fix it straight away.
B. He could have been annoyed and reprimanded the manager.
C. He could have done both the above.
D. He could choose to do none of the above.

He chose option D.

What he did instead is the crucial reason why Starbucks has such a successful and scalable business model.

He called the main operations lead for the whole organisation and asked what the process was to handle a light being out. By doing this he went to the source and he addressed the system rather than immediately applying a band-aid solution.

It is this mentality that creates game-changing results. By creating a mentality of systems for yourself, and then a culture of systems for the entire company, it will lead to a lot more consistency, control and scalability.

CHAPTER 10

SALES AND MARKETING

Sales and marketing are two separate and important parts that are key to the success of any business. Whilst they are different, the connection between them is important and they both share a common goal.

What's The Difference Between Sales And Marketing?

Marketing

- Marketing is the first step in the marketing / sales and customer life cycle.
- The primary goal of marketing is to look at the bigger picture and create campaigns that attract attention, interest and inform prospects of the company's products and services to the point where they would like to know more or make a purchase.
- Marketing focuses on targeting your ideal customer within the general public or larger groups of people, while sales targets smaller groups of people or subsets of the general public.
- Marketers use market research and analysis to understand the interests of potential customers.
- Marketing departments are responsible for running campaigns to attract people to the business brand, product, or service.
- Marketing focuses on the longer-term outlook of the products, services and success of the company.
- Marketing campaigns should be designed in line with the company's capacity and vision.
- Marketing campaigns can be costly: it is important to test and measure their success and then scale them to attract the required number of leads. Having too few leads can lead to failure and having too many leads that cannot be dealt with is a waste and unnecessary marketing cost that could be better utilised elsewhere in the business.

Sales

- Sales works directly with the prospects who were reached and attracted through the marketing to reinforce the value of the company's solution.
- Sales works to convert prospects into customers.
- Sales is a term used to describe the activities that lead to the selling of goods or services. Salespeople are responsible for managing relationships with potential clients (prospects) and providing a solution for them that eventually leads to a sale.
- Sales are required in order to make profit. The growth of your business is dependent on your profit. Without profit, your business cash flows will become unsustainable and you will not be able to successfully invest in new products/resources or hire new employees.
- It is always possible to be beaten by a competitor – even if you are offering the same product for a lower price. Sales should also focus as on the other features of your product and company in order to make the sale.
- Sales focuses more on the shorter-term goals and hitting quotas and volumes.
- Sales goals are often measured daily, weekly and monthly.

Marketing vs. Sales

While these two business functions may sound straightforward and simple, they are different components of a business that share a common goal. This is to attract prospects and convert them into paying customers who generate revenue and profit in addition to building long-term customer relationships.

A marketing, sales, customer lifecycle is as follows:

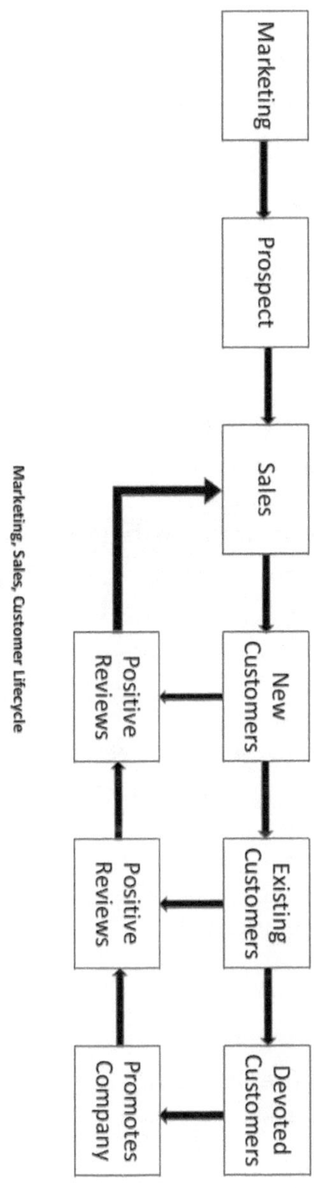

The diagram on the previous page illustrates the value and importance of creating positive customer experience and satisfaction, which translates into valuable word-of-mouth marketing and reducing overall marketing efforts and costs.

To create a cohesive partnership between marketing and sales, we first need to understand the core elements of each department. The first step is to look at developing a marketing strategy and plan.

Creating A Marketing Plan

A good marketing plan is a high-level plan that guides your team's campaigns, goals, and growth in the right direction to make your company's business goals a reality.

Without a plan, things can get messy and it becomes near impossible to prepare a budget for the marketing activities and campaigns.

Keep in mind there will be variations to the marketing plan, depending on your industry and the goals of your marketing team. To help you with creating this, I have compiled a list of what a high-level marketing plan will typically include.

Marketing Plan Elements

Regardless of whether you're selling to consumers (B2C) or other businesses (B2B), there are seven elements every effective marketing plan includes:

1. Marketing Summary

Your marketing plan summary should include:

- Company Name
- Marketing Leadership Team
- Headquarters, Office Locations
- Mission Statement
- SWOT Analysis

The information should be aligned with the main business plan and sales strategy.

2. Marketing Initiatives

The marketing Initiatives element of a marketing plan helps you segment the various goals of your department. This section of your marketing plan should outline the projects that are specific to marketing. Describe the goals of these projects and how these goals will be measured.

3. Target Market

If your company has already carried out a thorough market research study, this section of your marketing plan will be easier to put together.

This element of your marketing plan will help you describe:

- The market that you are selling to.
- An analysis of your competitors.
- Your buyer persona.
- Competitive analysis.

4. Marketing Strategy

Your marketing strategy uses the information included in your target market section to describe how your company should approach the market. What will your business offer your buyer personas that your competitors aren't already offering?

In a full-length marketing plan, this section can contain the "Seven Ps of Marketing". These Ps are product, price, place, promotion, process, people and physical evidence.

- **Product** – The physical characteristics of the product or service you are selling. It can include features, warranty, design and packaging, etc.
- **Price** – The pricing of your products/services should consider the prices of your competitors, discounts and profit margins. The 'gross profit margin' refers to the difference between the selling price of an item and the price that you paid for it or that it cost you to make.
- **Place** – This covers the distribution of your service/product. Factors to consider include where you are planning to sell (for example online or door to door, the delivery of your product and so on).

- **Promotion** – This covers how you communicate your product/service to your target market and includes your sales team, advertising, telesales, public relations and email marketing, newsletters, etc.
- **Process** – This refers to the service included with the sale of your product/service, such as performance standards, post-sales support, monitoring Key Performance Indicators (KPI).
- **People** – If you plan to have employees, consider what training and incentives you will provide and the team culture you are aiming to have.
- **Physical evidence** – Include details of results that have been achieved to date and how you achieved them, customer satisfaction results, etc.

Marketing teams can take different strategic approaches depending on the type of campaign and customer that are being targeted. Common marketing strategies include:

- Internet marketing.
- Print marketing.
- Blog marketing.
- Search engine optimisation.
- Social media marketing.
- Video marketing.
- Holding special events: grand openings, new product unveilings, contests.
- Free publicity: press releases, editorials.
- Networking: tradeshows, trade organisations, chambers of commerce.
- Create a referral system. Harness the power of word of mouth by rewarding customers for referring others.

5. Marketing Budget

Your marketing budget describes how much money the business has allotted the marketing team to pursue the initiatives and goals outlined in the elements above. It is important for the marketing team to prepare a budget based on what they would like to do and the results that they would expect to be achieved, rather than simply wait for a random sum to be allocated by the company for marketing.

It is always important to itemise the marketing budget by what you will specifically spend the budget on.

It is also important to remember that it costs far more to attract new customers than it does to maintain your existing client base, which is why it is important to monitor customer satisfaction. There are several ways to assess customer satisfaction such as:

- Talking to customers in person or on the phone.
- Survey feedback forms at events or by post.
- Email follow-up.
- Social media channels.
- SMS text message.

There are various ways to retain customers such as:

- Discounts.
- Competitions.
- Customer loyalty schemes.
- Keeping in regular contact through newsletters.
- Special offers and so on.

Always let your customers know and feel that you are really listening to them. If they're unhappy with something, don't be afraid to apologise or admit it and reassure them that you're taking steps to improve. By being honest, they will be more likely to respect you for acknowledging any shortcomings and appreciate the measures you take to make amends.

6. Marketing Channels

There are so many different marketing channels that exist today to reach your ideal customers that it can be confusing which ones to use. Rather than being everywhere, it is important to find and then focus on the areas where your customers are most likely to be. Include a list of the marketing channels you plan to use in your marketing plan, such as:

- Facebook.
- Instagram.

- LinkedIn.
- Pinterest.
- Twitter.
- Email.
- SMS text message.

80% of your leads are likely to come from 20% of your marketing efforts. Always be testing and concentrating on the 20% that is producing 80% of the results.

If you publish or intend to publish on social media, use the Marketing Channels section of your marketing plan to lay out which social networks you want to launch a business page on, what you'll use this social network for, and how you'll measure your success on the network.

Businesses with an extensive social media presence might even consider elaborating on their social strategy in a separate social media plan.

In the last few years, social media platforms have become more and more popular and the number of people engaging online has grown by a staggering amount. This phenomenon of online communication has escalated with technological advancements, such as smartphones and tablets, and can now be considered a vital marketing tool.

With so many social platforms, and most completely free to use, if used correctly social media is a cheap and easy way to communicate with customers. Things to consider:

Who is your target market?

What are their online habits and what are they talking about? Don't just join any and every site at random (although register on them all to protect your name and brand). Choose the ones that your customers are engaging on. For example, if you sell wedding stationery, you may want to set up a Pinterest profile where the majority of users are female and the 'virtual pinboard' design will provide a convenient way to display your products online.

I.   **Integration.**

Link your social media channels to your website to increase traffic and encourage customers to look around your site.

II.   **Let your company's personality shine through.**

While sales talk on social media platforms is good in small measures, it is better to focus more on providing valuable content, being personable, interesting and approachable.

III.   **Measure your success.**

Tools such as Google Analytics can be used to track conversions from your social media sites and identify how much your social media presence is benefitting your marketing and/or customer service strategies.

IV.   **Be relevant to your target market.**

An effective advertising campaign should target your potential and existing customers and not everyone. Tailor your message and offers to be relevant to your market and they will be perceived as more personalised.

V.   **Be appealing and memorable to your customers.**

Pay attention to the graphics and the layouts that you use. The images, colour and movement of your adverts will be the things that customers notice in the first few seconds of scanning your advert, so it's important to get and then keep their attention. Your copy should be easy to read, specific and believable. Content that is funny or thought-provoking is more likely to be remembered and shared among your audience. Remember to include the unique benefits of your product/services.

7. Tools and Resources

There are lots of new technologies being introduced that can be adopted to make marketing much easier and more efficient.

The introduction of resources to a marketing or sales strategy is particularly dependent on new technology. For example:

- A.I. and live chat are new tools that can be used in marketing and sales to develop relationships with leads.
- A CRM system is a tool that can be used by sales, marketing, and the company as a whole. The database helps all departments manage relationships with contacts, no matter which stage of the customer lifecycle they are in.
- Social media can be leveraged for marketing.
- Social media can be used to promote content.
- Social media can be used for sales and as part of a social selling strategy.

Reviewing Your Marketing Plan

Similar to your business plan, you should refer to this on a regular basis and keep it updated, reviewing which goals have been achieved, which strategies are working and which areas may need more work. You should also update your plan to reflect any changes in your target market or customer preferences.

Sales Strategy

If you think of sales in terms of solving a problem, then the concept of selling doesn't need to be scary. It is important to remember that selling is serving and if you are confident that your product or service can solve a problem and offer your potential customer value, then you are doing a disservice by not offering them your solution to help them.

Sales is about explaining and showing your prospects how purchasing a product or service from your business will benefit them and help them solve a problem. When you can do this effectively, you will soon build their trust.

Here are some strategies for creating a sales system within your business:

- Develop a sales technique and process (e.g. creating rapport, asking detailed questions, empathising with their concerns) and train your team members to use them consistently.
- Track conversion rates. The difference between the number of

enquiries you receive, and the number of actual sales achieved is like taking the sales pulse of your business.

- Include cross-selling, up-selling and bundling products together.
- Have a follow-up system in place. Up to 80% of sales are made after the 5th contact.
- Set up an annual promotion schedule to maintain a consistent and constant sales and marketing programme. Each of your customers needs to feel important, cared about and valued. If they feel that you're uninterested or indifferent to their custom, they can easily be tempted to look elsewhere and be lured away by a competitor. On the other hand if they have been impressed with your service, not only are they more likely to tell their friends, family and colleagues about the wonderful experience they had, they are also more likely to adopt the familiarity principle and return as a loyal customer, expecting the same great service. Why would they shop around elsewhere when you've already delighted them?

Having the right sales strategy will make or break your business.

How The Best Businesses Are Creating Winning Sales Strategies

Sales plans include details about the sales process, sales team structure, target market, and goals. Plus, the sales plan outlines the actions, tools, and resources that will be used to hit these targets.

Like marketing strategies, there are also sales methods that can be adopted depending on the industry, products, market, and target customer. Some of the most popular sales methods are:

- SPIN Selling – SPIN stands for: Situation questions, Problem questions, Implication questions, Need questions.
- Solution Selling – focuses on the customer's problems and addresses the issues with appropriate solutions (product and services).
- NEAT Selling – NEAT stands for: Need, Economics, Access, Timeline.
- Conceptual Selling – deals with the prospect's concept of a product or service and relates it to the prospect's issues.
- SNAP Selling – is designed to help your prospect focus on these

decisions and then agree to what you're proposing as solutions. The SNAP system highlights four factors: keep it simple; be invaluable; always align; raise priorities.

- Customer-centric Selling – makes customer satisfaction a priority value; puts customer satisfaction ahead of everything else; rewards employees for customer satisfaction; gets everyone involved with the customers.
- Inbound Selling – is a personalised, helpful, and modern sales methodology that focuses on the prospect's pain points and adapts the sales process to the buyer journey.
- MEDDIC – stands for: metrics, economic buyer, decision criteria, decision process, identify pain, champion.
- The Challenger Sale – The Challenger Sales Model is an approach to sales that is tailored to how the Challenger teaches, tailors, and takes control.
- The Sandler System – allows sales reps to build up mutual trust by asking questions to determine whether the solution being offered is the right fit for the client.

Some sales strategies come and go with the release of the latest bestselling book or the launch of new tools and technologies. Others are firmly rooted in psychological principles that are here to stay and explain what really motivates people to buy or not buy.

25 Effective and Proven Sales Strategies That Can Be Employed:

1. Always lead with what's in it for your prospect.
2. Build rapport and trust before selling.
3. Perfect your sales pitch (make it exciting and amusing, to be memorable).
4. Clearly articulate end results – if you confuse them, you will lose them.
5. Sell based on tapping into your customer's emotions and then justify the sale based on logic.
6. Use storytelling to engage your customer and bring them on a journey.

7. Use lead scoring to prioritise your prospects.
8. Connect with the decision maker straight away, or as quickly as possible.
9. Be flexible when faced with new challenges or objections. Keep a record of them.
10. Listen to what your prospects are telling you.
11. Give your undivided attention to your prospect.
12. Negotiate for a win-win.
13. Always follow up until you get a definitive answer.
14. Highlight the risks and opportunities.
15. Develop the right mindset.
16. Always be helpful.
17. Ask for specific referrals.
18. Give short product demos.
19. Reach out to qualified leads within 24 hours of sign-up.
20. Address uncertainty when you see it.
21. Use the PAS framework – PAS stands for **P**roblem-**A**gitate-**S**olution.
22. Create a sense of urgency.
    a. Limited availability.
    b. Limited time period.
    c. Not for everyone.
    d. Upcoming price increases.
    e. Custom offers.
23. Sell more to your existing customers.
24. Intelligently use free trials.
25. ABC – **A**lways **B**e **C**losing.

Sales and Marketing Alignment

It is important to have your sales and marketing plans and strategies aligned with each other and the overall business plan, with a smooth and well-defined transition between them.

A good way to form a harmonious partnership between the sales and marketing teams is to create a service level agreement that defines their shared goals, identifies the buyer personas or ideal client profile, standardises lead definitions, sets out a protocol for lead management, and outlines how sales and marketing performance will be measured.

At the end of the day, you can try all the sales and marketing strategies in the world, but the best way to improve your lead generation and sales rate is through real experience. There's no substitute for trial and error. Learning what you can from every interaction and developing an understanding of what motivates your customers to buy or not buy will help you refine the best marketing and sales strategies.

When sales and marketing are aligned with each other and your target market, the business is perfectly positioned to attract and qualify more leads and generate more revenue through sales. The diagram below illustrates the relationship and where you need to focus your attention in developing your products, marketing and sales.

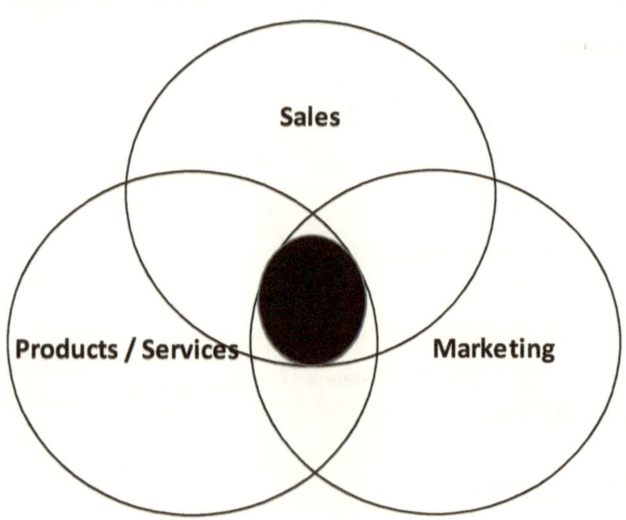

CHAPTER 11

SUPPORT

All businesses start with great hope, enthusiasm and intentions. However, a large percentage of businesses fail and most of those who manage to make it past the first few years are merely managing to survive rather than thrive.

There are only a small percentage of businesses that truly succeed and offer the owner the freedom to work on the business rather than in the business. It's probably only 1% to 3% of businesses that make it into this category. There are many different reasons for this, and it generally comes down to a lack of business knowledge, skills and support and not the lack of ideas and solutions to solve problems and fill needs.

Having an open and growth mindset and the ability to adapt is essential to building a successful business.

Here are some of the top reasons as to why businesses fail:

- No support or lack of support.
- No market demand for products or services. Maybe the demand is there, but the marketing strategy is wrong.
- Poor financial management and running out of cash. Some companies are profitable but still fail due to this.
- Not the right team running the business.
- Outperformed by the competition.
- Pricing and cost issues.
- Poor products and/or services.
- Lacking a solid business model.
- Poor marketing.
- Poor customer services / relations – ignoring their customers' needs or concerns.
- Scaling too fast and running out of cash.
- Failing to innovate and being complacent regarding future trends.

- Ego-driven greed. Short-term thinking.

The truth is that there really is only one reason why businesses fail and it's generally never what the business owner wants to hear when it happens! The reason is always due to the owner. We all have our strengths and weaknesses. When we look into this deeper, it comes down to not having the right support in place to build our knowledge and skills to maximise our strengths and to put in place measures to strengthen our weaknesses and keep us on-track when things occur that we do not have the knowledge and skills to handle. If we delve another level deeper, it can usually be discovered that it comes down to the CEO not having an open and growth mindset. They knew it all already!

Blockbuster video would be an example of this. They failed to adapt to the changing market and were destroyed by the competition. There are many business lessons that can be learned from the Blockbuster's rise and fall. This is also a good example of an opportunity reaching its expiry date. If Blockbuster had adapted to the changing market, they could have used their existing dominant market position to thrive. Instead, they believed in their strength over the competition and ended up struggling to survive and, ultimately, going out of business.

> *"It is not the strongest companies that will always survive, it is the ones that are able to adapt to the market and use their existing strengths to thrive and keep the new competition from scaling."*
> **– Calum Kirkness**

It is never the economy. Most business failures at the moment get blamed on Brexit and the mainstream media are happy to go along with this as it meets their narrative of Brexit not being a good thing. Periods of change provide the greatest opportunities and periods for an entrepreneur to thrive in. When your customers and competitors are watching the news and following the mainstream media and feeling fearful, seek the courage to take the opportunities and take the opposite direction to the masses.

Some entrepreneurs who fail realise it was due to their own mistakes and they will bounce back more knowledgeable and experienced than ever before. This is a great quality. With this type of mindset, there really is no failure, there is only ever a gift or a lesson.

We all have blind-spots and, as I mentioned earlier in the book: we know what we know, we know what we don't know, but we don't know what we don't know. Successful people have an open, positive mindset and are always looking to grow and bounce back; the poor have a closed mindset and think they know it all already, which will keep them stuck in employment thinking it's the low-risk option or if they do start will likely end in failure, which will put them back into employment. I am sure you have come across people who fall into these categories.

Here are a few of my top tips for having the right support and network to help you succeed:

- Have a coach or mentor.
- Attend masterminds with other successful entrepreneurs.
- Don't be shy to share your problems. Others in your team or supply chain are likely to be able to offer you support.
- Be willing to support and help others with your strengths and knowledge and they will be keen to reciprocate in future to help support your areas of weakness with their strengths.
- Don't look to seek answers from family and friends who don't understand the problem. They may be able to offer help in the form of feedback on products and services, and how to reach potential customers (as they will all be consumers themselves) but don't ask them for advice on business strategy if they are employees.
- Attend training seminars and events, both free and paid.
- There will usually be some government agencies in your area that offer business support and training events.
- Be careful who you are taking advice from. For example, if you go to your local government small business support agency, you may be speaking to an employee who has never run their own business. If you attend one of the events, it is also important to consider if the training is being delivered by someone who has actually run a business

themselves and they are sharing their knowledge and experience, or just an employee who can only share their knowledge. Knowing something and being able to do it are two completely different things.

- Always keep an open mindset for learning new information. Everyone can learn something from everyone else regardless of the level of intelligence, knowledge, experience or success.
- Some of your greatest supporters will be people that you don't know and some of your biggest haters will be people that you know well.

When running a business, never be totally hands off. I have seen CEOs of large companies step back from their business operations due to ill health or wishing to take a break, only for their business to quickly go into decline. They may appear to have not been doing much, but simply their presence and vision and checking in was enough for everyone to feel safe in the company and committed to the brand and vision.

Another thing I have seen is when a CEO decides to sell their business to a new owner or competitor, the business can go into decline quite quickly. You might question how one person can have such a large influence when the company becomes a huge organisation, but it does happen. I have seen some CEOs of large companies sell their business and be so hurt at watching its decline that they buy it back and turn it back around in a short period of time.

No one knows your business and vision like you do. No one will be more committed to give your business the edge in terms of passion and vision than you are.

One person can give the whole market, the whole supply chain and the whole workforce the feeling of security in the company and brand. This will always come down to just a few key and strong, core values that the CEO consistently shows and is always rippling throughout the whole workforce – this also demonstrates that simplification is the ultimate sophistication. If you really want to know the CEO of a company, meet and speak to the workforce.

One error of judgement from the CEO or a member of senior management of a company can also lead to a company's demise.

There is a well-known example of how not understanding the power of a brand and the impact the media can have on the consumer: the CEO of the Ratner Group, Mr Gerald Ratner made what has now become an infamous speech at a conference of the Institute of Directors at the Royal Albert Hall on 23 April 1991.

At the time, the Ratner Group was a large group of successful jewellery companies. During his speech, Gerald Ratner referred to a set of cut-glass sherry decanters with six glasses on a silver-plated that they sold as being "total crap", which was the reason they could sell them for £4.95p.

He further compounded the remark by going on to say how they sold earrings, that cost less than an M&S prawn sandwich, but probably would not last as long.

At the time, the speech got a few laughs from the audience, but Gerald Ratner certainly wasn't laughing with what was to ensue afterwards.

Just a few wrong words in his speech would cost him his position as CEO of the company, the value of the company would plummet by around £500 million, which very nearly resulted in the collapse of the business.

It is said that his wife advised him not to include and make the jokes in his speech beforehand, but he didn't listen.

It is a great example of the power of words and how the mainstream media are ready to pounce on anything that they can use to bring about your downfall. Negative news attracts far more readers and spreads much quicker than good news or good comments and actions. Public speaking is an art and one that can add significant value to your business and building up your brand when used intelligently.

Today, Ratner's speech is still notorious in the corporate world as an example of the value of branding and image over quality. A business publicity disaster or marketing faux pas is often referred to as, "Doing a Ratners."

Mr Ratner bounced back from his failure by becoming a successful businessman again, which is the sign of a great leader.

It can take years to build a brand and reputation and only minutes to destroy it.

This story demonstrates the power of words and the importance of having good communication skills to engage people and bring them on a journey with you. It also highlights the range of skills required to build and run a successful business.

Everyone is human and we all have strengths and weaknesses. Use your strengths and reinforce your weaknesses with the right support.

CHAPTER 12

STANDING OUT

Being able to stand out in a positive and unique manner is a great way to beat your competition and achieve growth and success in your business. While most people understand the concept, many businesses fail to put this into practice for various reasons. These may include: thinking that they lack the knowledge to get it right or having a fear of what people will think.

The best way to stand out is to disrupt the market by doing something unique, funny or entertaining, which may even involve making a fool of yourself. Richard Branson and Virgin are great at coming up with ideas to attract people's attention and become memorable. There is a fine line between achieving positive and negative results.

The important thing is to get people knowing and talking about you, your business and your products and services, which is where good marketing and branding comes in. The message needs to be attractive, clear, identifiable and memorable.

It is now easier to reach more people with your marketing than ever before, but the competition is fierce. It has never been harder to get your message seen and heard. Your potential customers are getting bombarded with so much information and offers, it is hard to get their attention and be memorable.

In the beginning, standing out comes down to marketing. Your customers must know you exist, what you do and offer, and what your values are. The more you stand out, the more you will attract the customers you want and repel the ones that are not for you.

There are a lot of companies spending large sums of money on researching the market and studying the behaviour and psychology of consumers to get the edge on their competition. Despite the level of in-depth studies that some companies are going to, I think the truth is that most of their marketing is still a lot of trial and error. There are some basic marketing principles that are easy to follow though and when you add your own creativity, they can be highly effective and carried out on a relatively-low budget.

I like to keep things simple. Simple is the ultimate sophistication – and rather than spend large sums of money on research and fingers-crossed marketing, we just need to look around us and observe what works in terms of attracting people's attention. It is also a good idea to observe what attracts your own attention and, if it does, it will most likely do the same for other people. You can then use these insights as the inspiration to fuel your own marketing strategies and campaigns.

I have included some of my observations on branding and marketing in this chapter.

Example of branding a business:

Let's assume that you are a haulage company. You have just started your business with two trucks which are both different colours: one is white, the other is red, and the trailers are blue but also a bit rusty. You want to keep your audience as wide as possible and not miss any opportunities, so you call the company ABC General Haulage and you have the company name on the front side and rear of all the trucks for advertising. You haven't created a logo yet and you are delaying painting both the trucks in your brand colours because you are trying to save money. Do you think you will stand out and anyone will take much notice? Probably not.

Now, let's say that one of the things that you are passionate about is performance cars and you decide that you would like to specialise in transporting performance cars around the world. So you call your company PCT Performance Car Transporters Worldwide and have the trucks painted in your brand colours. The company name and the words "Worldwide Safe, Secure Performance Car Transportation", along with an image of a Lamborghini, Ferrari, and McLaren car, are printed across the front, sides and rear of all your trucks. Your drivers are in quality company-branded clothing. Do you think you are more likely to get noticed now? I think so!

The message is clear and easily identifiable. So, for a one-off upfront cost, you can have your company advertised for free as your trucks travel around. Because you are passionate about what you do, this will shine through in your message and everything that you do. As a result, you will make the right connections much easier and people will want to do business with you.

If we look at Eddie Stobart Logistics, this transportation company started from small beginnings with two trucks painted in the owner's favourite colours and this has now expanded to around 2,200 trucks, as well as expanding into rail, aviation and warehousing. All their trucks are easily identifiable and stand out in the company colours. Every truck has a woman's name, which is written on the cab of the truck. Because of this, they have created a 35,000-strong club of fans who go around the country spotting the trucks and sharing and talking about them with other fans. The drivers are always dressed smartly in branded workwear; the trucks are always clean and well driven at optimum speed for fuel efficiency. These are all values created and passed down by the company founder. The business has regularly featured on television and had its own series, as well as regularly appearing in other media outlets.

You can see how Eddie Stobbart Logistics has created a simple, yet effective, strategy that is followed with precision to create a brand that stands out above the competition.

Human beings tend to overcomplicate things. Remember that 80% of your marketing success will come from 20% of the efforts. Whilst bigger companies are out there spending millions of pounds on marketing, stick to focusing and working on the 20% of your marketing efforts that will get you 80% of the results. Observe what the large brands are doing and use this as inspiration to create your own strategies based on modelling their success.

Richard Branson is a good example of someone who is a master at doing things that make his personal and company brands stand out. He has a brand that is followed consistently and then spices it up with crazy, surprising acts to grab attention.

An important question to ask yourself is: "What makes my business different?" Why should a customer buy from you instead of your competition? If you have a tough time answering any of these questions, you have some work to do.

Here are a few ways to make your business stand out from competitors:

1. Provide legendary customer service.

Treat your customers like royalty. There are plenty of businesses that say they have outstanding customer service. However, just saying it is not enough. Actions speak louder than words.

All customers expect to receive good customer service and will not put up with anything less. Competition is fierce, and your customers won't stay customers for long if you don't take active steps to make them feel valued and build their loyalty. An example of a large company that offers great customer service is Amazon. There are also many small companies who offer much better customer service now than previously, as they have discovered the value of this in creating customer loyalty.

Everyone can make mistakes. The sign of a good company is not that they do not make any mistakes, but how they handle the situation when they do. Admitting mistakes and fixing problems with exceptional customer service can even end up strengthening the relationship.

Customers equate experience with brands. If they have even one bad experience that remains unresolved, they will write off the brand. Negative feedback will more than likely follow and spread like wildfire through social media and word of mouth. It's always important to be on top of your game in terms of customer experience.

This book is based around building a business that runs like clockwork and frees up your time, but there is one important distinction to make here. This is that you should never take your finger off the pulse when it comes to customer care and the finances. Things can quickly go AWOL when the owner leaves their businesses to run on autopilot. Although it is important to build a business that functions well without your continual presence, it is important to find a way to be the face of the business and connect with your customers. Thriving businesses all have the same thing in common: owners who are active and are engaged both inside the company and out in the community. At a small level, this is what I was referring to with my grandfather and how he was a good people and community person, which was very important to the customer experience and success of the business.

2. Offer great products and services that solve customers' problems and pains.

If you want to beat your competition, one of the best small business strategies you can employ is simply providing outstanding products or services. Word of mouth is a key influencer in purchasing decisions. If your product or service doesn't leave a positive lasting impression, you're not going to succeed in gaining loyalty, repeat customers, and new customers from referrals and word of mouth.

From doing market research in your niche, you will be able to identify gaps in the market where your competitors are missing opportunities and you will then be able to develop strategies for solving them. Creating outstanding products and services, backed up by outstanding customer service to fill the gaps, will help to separate you from the rest.

I have witnessed a good example of this over the last 15 years whilst spending a lot of my time in Malaysia. During one of my first visits there, whilst staying at a luxury 5-star resort, a local restaurant was recommended to me. When I first arrived at the restaurant, it didn't stand out at all. It had a large sign above the premises, but there was no consistent branding and it didn't look visually appealing apart from the fact that it was full of people. There were plastic tables, chairs and plates – it wasn't a place you would expect to be referred to by a 5-star resort. I didn't take long to realise that the restaurant had something special, which came down to a few key things. The customer service was exceptional, the food was delicious, the value was incredible, and these things were delivered with consistency. Every time I visit, the experience is the same. The same restaurant still exists today, totally unchanged and is full every evening with queues forming at peak periods from 6pm to 9pm. By sticking to the key components of what the customer is looking for when visiting a restaurant, they are full every evening based on word of mouth alone. The restaurants around them start up and close. Same location, but they cannot survive. This example demonstrates a few key things in business:

- Word of mouth is extremely important.
- The customer experience is extremely important.
- The products and services need to be exceptional.
- The value must be good.
- The service must be consistently good every time.

The restaurant has no marketing costs as their products and service sell themselves and the customers do the marketing.

This also shows that a nice shop front might grab people's attention the first time, but if the products, service or value are not there, they will not come back and you must continuously market to get new customers.

3. Develop unique-value products.

Your customers need to feel they are receiving *value* from what makes you different from the rest of your industry. This means either making your products and/or services better, having better prices, or simply offering more value. Competing on price alone is a tough game to enter and will usually end up in a race to the bottom. One way to stand out from the competition is to offer a guarantee that is better than your competition or industry standard.

By offering exceptional guarantees, you reduce the perceived risk of buying your products or services – and anything that you can do to eliminate the hesitation for your customer will lead to increased sales. A guarantee can also make your company seem more trustworthy and likable. A great example of this that I have observed over the years is in the car industry where the period and terms of warranties have increased from one year and low mileage limits to a general industry standard of three years and 60,000 miles, and now, three years and unlimited for some. Hyundai has also raised the bar above the whole of the market and started offering five-year unlimited mileage warranties on their new vehicles. Their market share and brand has increased in the last 10 years due to their strategy. Now Kia offers a seven-year 100,000-mile warranty and is becoming an increasingly recognised and growing brand as a result.

A free trial or money-back guarantee will also help assure customers they're receiving a product or service worthy of parting with their hard-earned money. Many businesses fail to recognise the power of this marketing tactic. If you are the only one in your niche offering competition-beating warranties, you will be sure to stand out and acquire more sales.

Another way to be unique is to offer free bonuses. People love freebies and value is everything.

4. Focus on a narrow niche.

When you try to serve everyone, you serve no one.

Many small business owners make the mistake of trying to appeal to a broad audience. Small businesses are better to target specific groups with precision: groups that are looking to solve a very specific problem. When you define your target market and understand who benefits the most from your products or services, you'll be able to attract more customers and charge more for your specialisation and perceived value. For example, think of a heart surgeon compared to a general doctor. The market for a heart surgeon is much smaller than for a general practitioner (GP) but the problem that they solve is much bigger as is the reward that they receive.

I remember hearing a story about a motorbike mechanic debating their worth with a heart surgeon. The motorbike mechanic was saying that they both do a similar job in that they both "fix the engine" so their pay should be equal. The heart surgeon thought for a moment and nodded his head in agreement, before he replied, "Yes, that is correct: we both do a similar job. But in my job, I must fix the engine whilst it is still running." This is a humorous example to illustrate the difference in the problem that the customer has and the value that you can bring to them.

5. Define your brand.

Having a great company name, eye-catching logo and smart merchandise is a great starting point in creating a good impression. We don't get a second chance to make a first impression.

We can "speak loudly by speaking visually" as demonstrated in the example given about Eddie Stobbart and his haulage business.

The chart below provides you with insights into the psychology of colours, with some examples of the colours being used by famous brands.

COLOUR PSYCHOLY CHART FOR VISUAL BRANDING

Colour	Postive / Negative	Emotion					Famous Brands					
Red	+	Power	Excitement	Strength	Passion	Energy	Coca Cola	Lego	Virgin	Toyota	Mcdonald's	KFC
	-	Danger	Warning	Anger								
Orange	+	Confidence	Courage	Innovation	Friendliness	Success	Fanta	Amazon	Harley Davidson			
	-	Ignorance	Sluggish									
Yellow	+	Optimism	Warmth	Happiness	Creativity	Friendliness	McDonalds	Shell	Ferrari			
	-	Unstable	Irresponsible									
Green	+	Health	Hope	Nature	Growth	Freshness	BP	Land Rover	John Deere			
	-	Jealousy	Envy	Guilt								
Blue	+	Trust	Loyalty	Dependability	Logic	Security	Facebook	Twitter	Samsung	Ford	American Express	Dell
	-	Masculinity	Coldness	Fear								
Purple	+	Wisdom	Luxury	Wealth	Spirituality	Sophistication	Cadbury					
	-	Mystery	Moodiness									
Pink	+	Imaginative	Passionate	Transformation	Balance	Creativity	Barbie	Victoria's Secret				
	-	Femininity	Immaturity	Weak								
Brown	+	Serious	Earth	Reliability	Authenticity	Conservative						
	-	Conservative	Dogmatic									
Black	+	Sophistication	Security	Power	Authority	Substance	Nike	Puma				
	-	Death	Evil	Mystery								
While	+	Cleanliness	Clarity	Purity	Simplicity	Freshness						
	-	Pristine	Isolation	Emptiness								
Balanced	+	Neutral	Calm	Balanced			Apple	Honda				
	-	Balanced										
Diversified	+	Mixed feelings					Microsoft	Google	eBay			
	-	Mixed feelings										

WWW.CALUMKIRKNESS.COM

On a deeper level, your brand is so much more than graphics. Your brand should act as a constant reminder to current and potential customers of why you are different and better than your competitors – and should not just communicate what makes you unique, but *magnify* it.

The best way to stay memorable is to go against the crowd.

Branding takes time to insert into a potential customer's mind. So, there is a need to go the extra mile. Do stuff your competitors don't want to do.

From your social media and general marketing message to the visual elements of your company and your interactions with customers, these all help shape your business and the credibility you hope to obtain.

6. Become a brand advocate.

The best salesmen aren't necessarily the best businessmen. There are many forms of selling, and being an advocate for your brand combines many of them into one cohesive message.

If you're passionate about your business, share your passion with others and make them excited about your business too. Make sure others understand the story behind the products, the people they have helped, your company mission, and so on. By doing so, you'll become an authority in your niche and stand out from the pack. Think of the example I shared earlier regarding the new haulage business: if the owner of ABC General Haulage was speaking to customers, he would be unlikely to come across as a brand advocate, but if he was talking to people about PCT Performance Car Transportation, he most likely would. This is also a good example of why you should do what you feel passionate about.

7. Become an expert.

To truly beat your competition and separate yourself from the pack, you need to position your business as the go-to experts by demonstrating your uniqueness and expertise, and providing your target audience with a reason to reach out to you and purchase your product or services. You could have the best offer in the world, but customers won't come back if they don't find you credible as an expert in your field. Get to know your industry inside out and be willing to share that knowledge. This level of credibility is what builds consumer trust and it's this kind of trust that will get customers to refer others to your business.

8. Create an amazing and memorable company culture.

As well as building the company to stand out and be attractive to customers, measures should also be taken to make the company attractive to work for and attract the top talent. A great way to think about this is: how can I turn my company into a place where people look forward to Monday mornings as much as they do Friday afternoons? There are many things that can be done to create a positive work environment.

When a customer is served by a happy employee, the experience for the customer is enhanced, which enhances the experience for the employee and a positive cycle is created. This can act as a positive marketing tool as your employees become brand ambassadors that help promote your company.

What can you do to make your company a place that people want to go to on Monday mornings?

9. Contribute to a good cause.

Giving back by lending the company's time, money and expertise to help promote non-profit organisations in the community is a good way to contribute to a good cause in addition to helping your business build its brand awareness and credibility based on shared values.

10. Become a social business.

If you want to take your corporate giving to the next level, you could take your efforts one step further to become a social business.

There are more and more companies cropping up that have this kind of approach.

This approach might mean making a dramatic shift in your entire business model, but these businesses stand out because they are not just another company, they are making a positive impact on the world with every sale.

11. Build your professional and personal profile.

This involves doing a bit of a PR job on yourself and investing time. Find some ways to get your name out there by being on social media and contributing to industry publications, arrange interviews for podcasts, speak at conferences, start a blog or vlog, etc.

Establish yourself as a thought leader in your niche and don't shy away from promoting your publicity.

Creating a great social media presence is important and a good way to reach people – you never know who is watching! The average person spends nearly two hours on social media each day, so if you are not using it to remind people that you exist, you are missing out on a big opportunity. Make sure your profile is consistent across all channels and try them all to see which ones you get the most engagement on. Then, select a few to concentrate on.

12. Build strong relationships by communicating well.

Everyone knows customer relationships affect the success of your business, but few understand *how* impactful loyalty is. Some studies show around 90% of customers stop doing business with a company after they have experienced poor service.

It is important to try to stay in contact with prospects and customers on a regular basis, at least once a week, by sharing your knowledge and giving them tips, discounts and so on to get to know your business. Even if they don't open your emails, or whatever way you communicate with them, your messages will get noticed and some will get read. Some people may even look forward to receiving and reading what you say.

It's also important to get customer feedback on your products and services. The information is invaluable in helping you improve your products and services and developing strong customer relationships. It can also provide you with the information to develop new products and services to meet their needs.

Also take the opportunity to surprise and delight your customers, employees and supply chain. Send thank you notes to customers, employees and supply chain partners who you are enjoying working with for good service. These little things really can go a long way in building strong relationships. Send them a small gift.

Think about every touch point that you have with the customer to use your creativity to stand out.

Show yourself to be a genuinely nice person.

Develop stories. Become a storyteller and practise your pitch at every opportunity – whether this is to investors, future team members, founders, friends, family and even partners.

If you want to stand out from the crowd, give people a reason not to forget you.

13. Build a community.

Building a passionate online and offline community is a great way to gain the trust and respect of current and future customers. It takes time and dedication to build, but it doesn't cost much.

Social media platforms are great for building online communities, and local events and workshops are great ways to grow an offline community.

14. Build a website.

We have all searched for a local business of some sort on Google and if you don't have a website for your company, you are missing out on a huge opportunity. Your website doesn't need to be fancy or expensive, but it should provide a nice, attractive and welcoming user experience. It should be consistent with your brand and have details about your company, what you do, and contact details. It must also be mobile-friendly as many people will be searching for the information from their smartphones.

15. Focus more on innovation.

When you go to all the effort to identify a niche in the market and stand out, it is important to continue to innovate and outperform your previous products at a faster pace than your competitors or your brand will go into decline and die. Winners focus on winning; losers focus on winners. The smartphone sector and the car industry are both good examples of innovation and continuously releasing new products – manufacturers are working on the next products before the current versions have even been launched.

16. Break the rules but not the law.

Doing the *opposite* of what everyone else is doing is a great way to stand out and be talked about. Conventional wisdom is often wrong, so challenge it – rewriting the rules of doing business in your industry can give you an advantage. It is important to make sure you aren't detracting from the value of your products and services with your ideas though or you end up scoring an own goal.

Conclusion

The chances are that you may have heard many of these small business marketing and branding strategies before, but many new and existing businesses are missing out by not putting them into action.

Visual marketing and word of mouth are powerful in terms of attracting customers, but it is your products, service and value that will keep them coming back and spreading the word.

These simple, time-tested tips can help you to stand out from the competition and dominate your niche.

CHAPTER 13

SCALING

What Does Scaling Your Business Operations Mean?

Scaling a business is not the same as growing a business. A company can be growing but not necessarily scaling.

For example:

Growing – when you sign a new contract with a new client you grow your revenue, but you also end up increasing and growing your expenses at the same rate. If every sale you make requires the same amount of time and effort as the previous sale, then your business model is not scalable.

Scaling - Companies can scale their business when they can increase revenues while their operating costs remain low. This happens when your business is able to cope with an increase in sales, work, or output in a cost-effective, reasonable manner. It does this while maintaining or increasing its efficiency and without suffering in other areas such as employee turnover due to heavy workloads or a product that can't be produced fast enough to meet demand.

How can you focus on quickly scaling your business while still building a strong organisation?

There must be the desire and willingness to scale the business

Most entrepreneurs want to grow their businesses, but many don't have the dream of growing the business past a certain point. Many entrepreneurs lack the ambition or belief to scale when they are in the start-up phase of their business. If scaling your business is a priority, then you must develop a plan and action steps for how this will be achieved.

Start Planning Before You Scale Operations

In order to develop a plan, it is important to have a clear picture and understanding of where the business is at and the level where you want to take it. Once you know the ultimate goal for your business, the focus needs to be on what you want to be and not what you are. The decisions you make as a £100k-a-year business are different to those of a business that turns over £1m, and they will be different again if you are turning over £10m. If you want to become a £10m business, you must start thinking like one.

It is also important to understand and keep in mind the exit strategy. For example, building a company to sell requires a different approach to growing a business that supports a lifestyle.

You Can't Scale What's Broken

Many entrepreneurs make the mistake of thinking that they are ready to grow and scale before they really are.

Before you start to scale up, it is important to audit what is currently taking place and where the strengths and weaknesses are. Identify any gaps in the current processes and fix them first – this needs to be a priority before scaling.

It is also important to understand that the processes that are already in place may not remain suitable as the business scales. As a rule of thumb, small start-ups work best with less rigid systems, rules and procedures and the bigger a company gets, the more rigid they need to be.

Once you've identified your endgame, the next step is to figure out what strategy will help you get there.

Steps to Scaling Your Business

1. Make sure you are ready and prepared for growth

When a business starts to scale up, things can begin to creak and any weaknesses get exposed. It is important to think carefully about how scaling up and growing your business will affect it. It is important to have robust processes ready and in place before scaling begins.

2. Learn from competitors who have successfully grown

Think about how they've done it by getting an understanding of their business model and learn the lessons of how they have succeeded. For example, finding out how many staff they have can give you an idea of how many you will need. Who are they selling to, where are they selling and how are they selling?

3. Identify milestones

It is important to identify milestones on the route to where you would like to be rather than just having one big end goal. It is important to also have a timeline in place and ensure that the rate of scaling is controlled and sustainable. Many small companies become the victim of attempting to grow too fast. Having milestones will help you to plan finances in terms of cashflow and funding requirements.

4. Identify your competitive edge

In order to scale your business, you need to clearly understand what sets you apart from your competitors in the eyes of your customers. You also need to understand the core strengths of your business so you can invest in focused growth.

5. Identify your ideal customer

Maybe you already know your ideal customer but are currently unable to supply all their needs – in which case the risk of scaling is reduced. However, you may be looking to target a new customer profile as you scale your business – in which case it is important to do your research in the same way that you did to identify your Ideal customer when starting out.

6. Optimise for the buyer

Once you've identified your ideal customer, speak to them and find out: what they want, need, what they care about, how they buy, and what processes they use. Once you understand their needs, it's time to optimise the building of your products and services around their problems with them at the centre. By putting your customers at the heart of your business, you will help attract and retain them and get them the results that they want. Make it easy for them to do business with you by making the sales cycle as short and simple as possible.

7. Protect your business values

The business values that helped create the solid foundations to scale up from should be safeguarded and protected. Things can change significantly when your business is growing and scaling up and there will be many things competing for your time and attention. It is important to be prepared for this.

8. Build a great team of employees

As you scale and grow your business, you are likely to need more staff. Your relationship with the new staff might not be as close as with previous team members, but everyone must realise the importance of your business values. Consistency and quality are paramount. Create the right culture and an environment where people want to be and want to excel – then get out of the way and let them get on with it. All team members must be properly engaged, motivated, recognised and rewarded.

9. Have rules for your staff to follow

I'm not talking about a strict regime, just something that guides. Having objectives and a strategy enables you to work out what talent you need. Recruiting the right people at all levels is essential to scaling up, and attitude is as important as skills and experience. People should be hardworking and ambitious. Everyone must pull in the same direction. Your employees should feel able to suggest improvements where possible. This can help your business to get better, stay current and grow.

10. Access outside expertise when required

A fast-growing business will soon exceed the point where the founders can grow it alone. When you reach this point, strategic advisors can help you push through this growth hurdle and get to the next step. That's because the right strategic advice will shortcut your learning curve and become a catalyst for growth. Strategic advice can be both formal and informal. For example, find people who *already* have the results you want and then arrange to meet for coffee. Use this opportunity to not only discover the strategies used, but find out whether they'd do it the same way again or if they'd take a different approach. This is a brilliant way to fast-track your growth.

11. Never compromise on quality or consistency

Quality and consistency are both required to enable and sustain growth. There's no point growing your business if your product quality or customer service deteriorates, because customers will start to go elsewhere. Having the right processes, culture and staff are key to maintaining quality throughout. You'll still make some mistakes when scaling, but understand why they happen, learn from them, get better and don't repeat them. A drop in values can lead to loss of existing customers. I have seen this take place many times and moved my business away from organisations where this has happened. One example where I did this was with professional advisors who were a small, family-run business, which had grown locally and managed to retain their values. They then had ambition to grow from local to regional level and started to buy other businesses in other areas. Due to the geography, a lot of the owner's time was spent travelling – which is generally unproductive and time-consuming. The result was that their focus was now taken away from the customer and on to the growth of the business. Due to the marked change in service that I experienced, I took my business away from them and transferred it to another business.

12. Identify your barriers to growth

Part of developing a strategy for scaling and growth involves thinking about possible barriers to scaling up. It is important to be honest about the factors that could hamper or prevent your ambitions to grow, such as lack of leadership skills, lack of funding, weak cash flow, wrong premises. By taking time to identify the potential barriers, you can have a plan and take action to help you address your weaknesses and potential threats before they become a problem that is hard or impossible to overcome.

13. Control finances closely and try to predict the future

Setting your business up to grow, doesn't always guarantee a smooth ride. No matter how good the plan is, you are still likely to experience some difficulties along the way. Having systems in place to help you spot something that isn't quite working means you can take evasive action to fix things before they escalate. When things go wrong, quite often it's because people have failed to recognise the signs, which can be evident months in advance. Stay particularly close to your finances: monitor your cash flow and measure your performance daily, which will give you hundreds of opportunities a year to put things right, rather than just 12 times if you only measuring performance every month.

14. Funding the scaling of the business

There are many different funding options and routes that can be taken. It is important to be cautious in whatever funding option you choose. Getting it wrong could end up with you paying a high price! It is always best to seek expert advice on assessing and negotiating the best option and deal.

Cash Is King

Before looking for external capital, businesses should always make sure they are managing cash effectively. Some simple steps can help maximise available cash, and being able to demonstrate good cash flow management sends out the right signals to potential investors or lenders.

The only way cash flow can be kept under control is by understanding it and closely tracking and forecasting it. A weekly cash-flow forecast is essential in a growing business. Management must have an understanding of the amount of cash and working capital required to operate the business as it scales. Examples of areas of the business that need to be carefully managed are:

- Stock and work-in-progress levels must be closely tracked and monitored, and active measures put in place to reduce excess stockholdings.
- Sales invoices must be issued in a timely manner through best-practice credit management procedures, with payments collected within the agreed set terms.
- Contractual agreements with suppliers should be reviewed to generate cash and ensure that suppliers are paid to credit terms.
- Capital expenditure should be carefully assessed, and consideration given to the cash-flow implications of making large purchases outright.

- Automated payment methods should be used wherever possible. Getting customers to pay by electronic transfer or through direct debit, helps increase the speed and certainty of receiving payments.

Cash management is not just part of the preparation for taking on new investment or debt, it is a procedure that must be ongoing. With any new stakeholders, the scrutiny of cash flow will likely be even greater as the business's journey proceeds.

There are generally two main categories of funding and then several different types within these categories:

Debt

- Family and friends.
- Bank loans and overdrafts.
- Peer-to-peer lending.
- Finance secured on assets.
- Leasing and hire purchase.
- Export and trade finance.
- Growth finance.

Equity

- Equity finance.
- Crowdfunding.
- Venture capital.
- Private equity.
- IPO – Initial Public Offering.

A word of warning: funding options all come with risks attached which can derail the growth plans of a business if they are not considered and managed appropriately. To make the most of them and keep the business safe, it is important to keep a very close eye on cashflow, cashflow forecasts and key cash metrics including debtor and creditor days, as well as gross profit margins.

As a rule of thumb, I would always look at debt as being the first option before considering giving up any equity within the company.

Before bringing in outside investors and giving up equity, it is advisable to explore all alternative options first so that you can retain control to grow your business the way you want. Investors often expect high returns, which can make bringing in investors the most expensive funding option. What's more, not only will you more than likely need to give up equity (and therefore control over your business – you could even find yourself being pushed out of your own company); there will also be more pressure due to the high expectations to deliver.

Overcome cash constraints creatively

Regardless of your scale strategy, you will need cash to fund your growth to help you implement the actions necessary to take you to the next step.

Lack of cash can be a big hurdle for growing businesses.

Options to consider when scaling a business are:

- **Creating a new revenue stream** – Introducing a steady recurring income steam, such as a monthly subscription model, is a smart strategy for any growing business. It's a good long-term strategy also. This model can also help you secure a higher sale figure for the business should you wish to sell in the future.
- **Joint ventures** – Working with someone else who already serves your ideal client is a quick and effective way to build your audience and create a greater pool of potential customers.

Scaling The Business

1. Start measuring success

As you scale operations, measuring all your processes individually and collectively is an essential part of your strategy, because it is the easiest way to keep track of where issues might emerge before they become major problems. Measuring and assessing should be a daily, weekly and monthly task for management. When issues arise during scaling, they should be addressed as swiftly as possible in order to avoid chaos arising, which can then become difficult to fix.

2. Focus on risk reducers

A risk reducer is any company attribute that reduces risk for the business, investors or customers.

By providing data-backed proof, your customers realise the benefits of your products and services and want to use them more. This is also good evidence to show investors. Having customer proof of greater market potential is a great indicator of success.

3. Focus on the right things

Entrepreneurs who are not able to scale their operations are usually focusing on the wrong things in their business. If you take a hands-on approach to your business (as I made the mistake of doing in the beginning of my journey), it can be very hard to scale your business.

In order to scale your business, there are three key areas to focus on:

- **Delegate** – you must focus on the key activities that will move your business forward in a strategic way, which requires being able to effectively delegate the responsibility for certain tasks to employees who are capable of performing them or may even be better at doing them than you! It Is important to understand when you need to delegate responsibility and ensure you don't get caught up in day-to-day items when your time could be better devoted to growing your business. Stay focussed on the 'big picture'.
- **Outsource** – outsourcing areas where you lack the skills, expertise or patience can be a great way to maintain a degree of flexibility whilst allowing you to focus on those activities which are in your zone of genius.
- **Automate** – one of the most effective ways to ensure consistency and efficiency in business processes is to automate them. Automation can eliminate most of the human errors that can affect the scaling of operations. It also reduces the amount of time that staff need to spend on these processes and allows them to focus on their core duties.

As the business scales, you will need to consider many different factors, top among them should be how to ensure the scaling is smooth and seamless for both staff and customers.

Flexibility and growth tend to go less hand in hand as the business gets bigger.

4. Build your network

Most entrepreneurs understand that developing your network and building the right connections are key to effectively scaling your business and long-term growth. Your network = your net-worth and much of business success comes down to who you know rather than what you know.

5. Don't hire salespeople or employees too early or too late

Recruiting is not always necessary or the right answer when it comes to the early stages of scaling and many businesses make the mistake of recruiting too early, before the company is ready. It is always best to ensure that the product and systems are ready and saleable before scaling. A better option sometimes is to outsource tasks and functions to retain a degree of flexibility and ensure the best medium- to longer-term outcomes.

The end goal for every business should be to create a product/service that is so good that it becomes the salesperson that speaks for itself.

The more phases of the sales process that you can take salespeople out of the better, which allows them to focus their time and attention on more valuable actions.

6. Keep It Simple

It can be both an exciting and scary time for a business when scaling. There is no shortage of strategies available that can be implemented, all of which claim to do magnificent things. It can be easy to get carried away with implementing additional processes, that add to complexity but give little results. The easiest way to maintain consistency in your business systems and processes is to keep them simple, especially during a time of change and flux.

It's also important to avoid spending too much time and money on new processes during the scaling-up stage and keep a degree of flexibility. It can be difficult to accurately predict what your needs will be in two years, never mind ten years' time. One of the last things you want to do is invest in processes that will hinder scaling of the operations in the future.

7. Mindset and performance

It is important that you have the right mindset and are doing the right things to ensure you are personally in the best position to run your company.

Focusing on your mindset, your health and wellness and your personal development as well as performance is key in order to scale successfully.

Questions to consider:

- What do you need support with in terms of mindset, health and wellbeing?
- What makes you feel good?

Scaling a business requires a whole new level of skills and systems that many entrepreneurs can't fully anticipate. For this reason, it is best to caution against scaling too quickly. Over 90 per cent of start-ups fail due to self-destruction, not competition.

CHAPTER 14

SAFEGUARDING YOUR BUSINESS

All business comes with an element of risk. If you want to be successful and wealthy, you not only need to know how to make money and build wealth, but you also need to understand how to protect and keep it once you have it. It is important to understand how you can do this by legally minimising the amount of tax that you pay, protecting the downside with the relevant insurances, ensuring you are operating in compliance with all the rules and regulations to avoid any penalties and fines, and protecting against internal or external fraud and theft.

"There are enough tools to play by the rules."
– Calum Kirkness

In business there are many rules and regulations to comply with and several licenses and permissions that may be required. Then there are insurances, some of which are mandatory, some highly recommended, and others desirable but not essential.

There are a lot of people in business who are operating in a manner that is non-compliant. Sometimes this is due to lack of knowledge and awareness, and this is where it is important to have a specialist power team in place to keep you advised and compliant.

Failure to comply with these rules, regulations and insurances can be costly and lead to criminal charges, fines, and other significant costs and problems. This can impact your business and wealth to varying degrees – sometimes as severe as losing everything that you have worked hard to create.

As you build up your business, it is important to adopt a wealth mindset and protect your interests and assets.

This chapter is a guide that looks at the main elements, permissions and protections to safeguard your business and wealth.

The ten key areas covered are:

1. Ownership/Control.
2. Controlling business finances.
3. Licences/registration/data protection/money laundering.
4. Protecting Intellectual property.
5. Rules and regulations.
6. Insurances.
7. Knowing who you are dealing with.
8. Ensuring your technology is secure.
9. Staying up to date with the news and competition in your industry.
10. Security.

1. Ownership / Control

Understanding the ownership of your business is a very important factor when it comes to how much control you have over the decisions that affect operations and strategy. If you own 51% or more of the voting rights of your company, you retain control over it. However, problems can arise if you relinquish more than 50% ownership when you are seeking external funding to grow the business. It can be a delicate balancing act when you have a great idea but no finance, and someone else has the finance required to start and scale the business. Without the correct knowledge, those with the great idea can find themselves ousted from the company and watch others reap the benefits of their idea.

2. Controlling business finances

It is important for any business to keep a tight rein on all finances. Failing to do so opens the door and provides people with opportunities to take advantage. Some of the basic control measures include things like:

a. Validate invoices before payment.
b. Check that goods or services have been received and there are no questions over quality, etc.
c. Check if an invoice is real and correct and hasn't been manipulated in any way.
d. Ensure you have dual release of payments set up. I hear of companies

where one person checks the invoices and pays them. Then, they wonder what went wrong when they finally notice thousands of pounds have been syphoned off. Always ensure two people are needed to get money paid out.

e.   Double-check you are paying the right people. Calling a supplier and validating their bank details is a simple process and should be followed, especially after you receive a letter asking you to change where or how a payment is made.

f.   Checking all transactions.

g.   Protect your credit! It is important to make sure your business has the best credit rating possible – this will ensure you can have access to finance in the form of a loan, credit from a new supplier, or increased credit from an existing supplier (if necessary). To protect your credit, make sure you pay your bills on time and don't let anything fall through the cracks.

h.   Don't show employees the money, show them the love. Show employees that you appreciate them and give them pay increases to reflect your appreciation. Showing your appreciation builds your relationship with them, which makes it more likely that they will show loyalty for you through thick and thin.

i.   Cut expenses. Regularly check expenses and look at ways to reduce them wherever possible. Some cuts can be obvious to spot, and involving your employees can help to spot others.

j.   Re-examine your credit terms. Keep a check on late-paying or non-paying customers and remind them that it is time for them to pay up. Set up payment plans, if necessary, and hold them to it. Or, as a last resort, take legal action to recover the debt.

k.   Manage your inventory. Keeping a close eye on your inventory will help conserve cash and keep the balance sheet clean.

3.   Licences, Registrations, Data Protection, Client Accounts and Money Laundering

When you are operating a business, there will be licences, registrations and data protection to consider, which will vary depending on the nature of your business and trading strategies.

Licenses and Registrations

- These will depend on the nature and geographical area of the business that you are operating.
- It is important to do your research and carry out checks that can be made with your local government departments.

Data Protection

Data protection has been big in the news recently, due to leaks of personal data by some large organisations. People are rightly becoming more and more sensitive to how their personal data is stored, used and secured.

All businesses that handle people's personal information must have compliance measures in place:

- The Data Protection Act 1998 requires every organisation or sole trader who is processing personal data to comply with the legislation.
- If you are not sure if you need to register, you can check online at: https://ico.org.uk/for-organisations/register/

Client Account

- A client account is an account at a bank in the name of the company to which it has been sent, but is separate from all other accounts linked to that company.
- If you receive or hold clients' money, then you must do so in accordance with the Clients' Money Regulations, 2012.

Money Laundering Regulations

Certain types of businesses are legally required to comply with Money Laundering Regulations. This involves carrying out 'due diligence' measures to ensure your customers are who they say they are. The most common types of businesses these regulations apply to include:

- Financial and credit businesses.
- Accountants.

- Tax advisors.
- Auditors.
- Insolvency practitioners.
- Casinos.
- Independent legal professionals.
- Estate agency businesses.
- Company formation agents.

4. Protecting Intellectual Property

Intellectual property is the product of original thought and endeavour and is what sets your business apart from your competition and can generate significant income and increase how much your business is worth.

The difficulty can be understanding what IP is, how it is of value to you, and knowing where to start.

People often get confused between the different ways that you can protect your IP. An easy guide to help you consider your options is:

- Trademarks help protect unique aspects of your business brand, such as name, logo or strapline.
- Copyright applies to things that you've created, like written or artistic materials.
- Patents protect new product inventions.

Trademarks

It is important to take steps to protect your brand(s) by registering trademarks in the countries where you offer your products or services. Once they are registered, it prevents other businesses from using them. Without them, your business is at risk of others imitating your brand and effectively stealing your goodwill. In the UK, IP rights, including trademarks, are registered with the Intellectual Property Office (IPO).

There are three key things to think about before applying for a trademark.

- First, check and ensure nobody else has got there first. A search on Google is a great place to start, but it's always a good idea to get professional advice also. An IP lawyer can search the right trademark registers before you pay for the application fee.

- Second, think about how recognisable your intended trademark is. The IPO won't register anything that isn't easily identifiable to the public, or words that simply describe the goods or services you're offering, if it contains offensive material, promotes illegal activities, or is misleading to the public in any way.

- Third, consider how valuable it is to you by asking yourself what the consequences would be if a competing business started using key elements of your brand without your permission. Without a registered trademark in place, there is nothing to stop them doing this. Securing trademark protection can offer peace of mind and enhance the value of the business.

Copyright

Copyright law protects your original written, artistic and musical creations.

Copyrights enable you to stop other people from using or copying your work without your permission. You don't need to apply to register your copyright work in the UK because, by law, protection will apply to your work as soon as you've created it.

It's common for businesses to find that people or competing businesses have copied and are using content from their articles, books, website, etc. One way to put people off doing this is to use copyright notices using the familiar © to show others that your content is copyright protected. While the © can be a red flag to others looking to steal your material, it doesn't give your work any additional protection over what you already have under copyright law.

If you do find that someone is infringing your copyright, you'll need to speak to an IP lawyer to send a "cease and desist" letter and potentially receive compensation. A letter can be enough to let them know that you are aware and to get them to stop and withdraw the material that they have copied.

Patents

Securing patent protection can be a complex, lengthy and costly process. The major hurdle during the application process is demonstrating that your invention is new. If you're successfully granted a patent, you'll have the exclusive rights to make and sell products that incorporate your patented invention for a period of 20 years. Having a patent can be invaluable to your business, particularly if it's an innovative invention that puts you ahead of your competitors.

With patents there are no reminders or notifications of any infringements. It is your responsibility to check these and take any actions necessary to protect them.

5. Rules and Regulations

With any business, there will be rules and regulations that must be complied with. The rules and regulations vary depending on the nature of the business and the geographical area that it operates in and covers. A good starting point to establish all the rules and regulations that will be applicable to your business is to carry out a search on the Internet and contact your local government departments who will be able to advise you or point you in the direction of the agency or agencies that can. There are far too many rules and regulations to include here, but here are just a few examples that will or may apply:

- Health and safety regulations (apply to all businesses).
- Trading standards.
- Operating hours.
- Planning consent – if you are planning to operate your business from your home.
- Planning consent and building control approval – if you are making alterations to a business premises.
- Plus many more. The way government departments tend to work, nothing gets made simpler; there are just further new rules and regulations that get added.

6. Insurance

Having adequate insurance in place to comply with the law and protect your downside is important for all businesses.

The numbers of claims being brought against businesses are on the increase as employees and consumers are more prepared now than ever to bring claims. The costs of defending these claims can be substantial, which is why it is important to consider having adequate liability cover in place.

To get the best advice on how to insure in line with both the law and the risks, a business should consult with a specialist insurance broker who is regulated by the Financial Services Authority and a member of the British Insurance Brokers' Association.

It is important to ensure that the company insurance policies are kept under review to be certain that they adequately reflect any changes in the business and the scale of risk that these changes have introduced.

The following section is a brief guide to the types of business insurance that are mandatory and those that are optional.

Essentially, business insurance falls into two categories:

- Mandatory.
- Optional.

There are three types of mandatory insurance.

- Any business that employs staff must have employer's liability insurance.
- Any business that runs company cars or vehicles must have motor insurance.
- Any business that operates in certain professions, such as the law, accountancy and finance, must have professional indemnity insurance.

There are many non-compulsory insurances that can cover things such as public liability, property, contents, equipment, interruption to business, stock, goods in transit, money, loan repayments, director's liability, professional liability for non-compulsory professions, product liability, partnership protection, health, critical illness and legal expenses.

Business Premises

A business will operate from premises of some description – whether it is a home office, commercial office space, warehouse, factory or a retail outlet.

A standard building insurance policy should offer insurance against damage caused by fire, floods, storms, lightning, vehicles, vandalism, explosions and riots.

Calculating the insurable value of a business building is not the same as the market value it would sell for and needs to be the full cost of reinstatement. To arrive at the reinstatement value of a building, a business should consult with a chartered surveyor in order to get an accurate figure.

If the property is leased, it will generally be the landlord who is responsible to insure the building. However, it is always best to check before signing any lease.

Property owners' liability insurance

If any members of the public visiting your business premises were to injure themselves and the property owner was at fault, the liability insurance would pay for any damages that they might claim as a result of winning their case.

Working from home insurance

Normal household insurance policies are not enough to cover people who run their business from home, and they will need to extend their household policies to include any office or business equipment.

If clients visit the property for business purposes, then, as with any business premises, public liability cover would also be required.

Contents insurance

Contents insurance should cover against fire, flood and theft and possibly accidental damage. There are usually two types of contents insurance to choose from. One is "replacement as new" regardless of age and condition, and the other is indemnity cover where the wear and tear to the item is deducted when the value of the claim is calculated. Some high-value items will need to be specified on the policy such as computer and printing equipment, mobile phones, etc. It is important to also ensure that equipment such as laptops is covered, both on and away from the premises.

Business interruption

Where a business suffers from fire, flood or major theft event that threatens to interrupt its ability to carry on trading, the insurance would provide cover for any costs or loss of profits that arise. The costs should include things like having to relocate to temporary premises and replacing or renting emergency replacement equipment.

Employers' liability insurance

Employers' liability insurance is compulsory for any business that employs staff. The aim is to provide the employer with cover to pay for any compensation or legal costs that arise as a result of a workplace injury or illness suffered by an employee that is deemed the fault of the employer.

Most employers' liability insurance policies now provide cover for up to £10 million.

It is important to have a copy of the policy displayed prominently in the workplace so that staff can read it and retain the copy of the insurance.

Public liability insurance

Many businesses have regular contact with customers or members of the public. Customers might visit the business. Public liability insurance is intended to cover any awards that are made against a business for any personal injuries or damage to property for which it might be responsible. The insurance also covers the legal costs and expenses involved in defending a business in case of any claims.

Public liability is by and large voluntary, although a few types of business must take out cover.

Businesses that visit clients should make sure that their policy provides both on- and off-site protection. As well as businesses that operate from a shop or office, those that are run from home might also need public liability insurance if clients are in the habit of visiting.

The cost of the premium will be determined by the nature of the business, the turnover and the number of staff employed.

Product liability insurance

Products must be made to a standard that suits their purpose. If a product causes personal injury or damage to property because it is faulty or defective, then the company that made or supplied it is legally liable.

Product liability insurance will provide cover for any awards that might be made against a manufacturer or supplier for any injury or damage that is the outcome of a defective product.

If the business that supplied a faulty product is separate from the business that manufactured it, then the supplier might actually find themselves more exposed than the manufacturer since it is often they who will be claimed against first.

Professional indemnity insurance

Provides cover for businesses that deal in knowledge or skills.

If the business makes a mistake or is negligent in some way, then it protects them against any claims for compensation from clients.

For many professional businesses, such as lawyers, accountants, financial advisors, it is compulsory; for architects, consultants, designers and the like it is advisable.

One important factor for professional indemnity insurance is that it must be held both at the time that the claim is lodged and when the mistake was made. This is because there is often a substantial time lag between the occurrence and the claim being made. In order to ensure that protection is in place, anyone who either retires or shuts down their business will need some form of continuation or 'run-off' cover.

It is always important to keep meticulous records for all projects or commissions, and contracts should contain detailed and clear definitions of the duties and responsibilities for all parties.

Directors' liability insurance

Being a director of a company brings with it additional responsibilities in a number of areas, which means you can be held liable individually, and collectively, over things such as health and safety, data protection, keeping adequate accounts, fraud and negligence.

Directors' liability insurance covers company directors for compensation, settlements and legal costs should a claim be brought against you.

Vehicle insurance

It is a legal requirement that all business vehicles must have insurance cover.

A business must also make sure that any employees' vehicles that are used for business purposes are also covered for business use.

Businesses with several vehicles may be able to get a discounted fleet insurance policy.

A business must also be aware of the previous driving convictions for anyone who drives any of the company vehicles and let the insurance provider know.

Goods in transit

Any business that transports goods should invest in insurance cover to protect them against damage, loss or theft while the goods are in transit.

Stock

Stock can be at risk when in storage to varying degrees, depending on the nature and location of the stock.

Money

Money in various forms can be covered against loss or theft. The premium will be priced based on the risk level and whether it is on the business premises, in a safe or in transit.

Business Travel

Anyone travelling while on business should have travel insurance in place.

Loan insurance

Businesses can take out insurance to protect their repayments on loans and overdrafts in case they are unable to meet their commitments, either though accident or sickness.

Legal expenses

Legal actions can be very expensive. Legal expenses insurance will cover the costs involved in conducting or defending a legal action and, depending on the policy, employment disputes, tribunals and tax audits.

Credit insurance

Should a customer be unable to pay a bill as a result of a business failure, the loss can be made good, wholly or in part, with a credit insurance policy.

Specialist insurance

Some specialist equipment machinery is expensive enough to require its own insurance policy. In some cases, and depending on the type of machinery involved, insurers will insist on inspecting the machinery involved on a regular basis.

Data processing insurance

Businesses that handle large amounts of electronic data can get insurance to protect their processing equipment.

Premiums

The cost of business insurance has become a thorny issue in recent years, with premiums reportedly rising by significant amounts each year. Insurers say the increasing willingness of employees to bring claims against their employers has added to the expense of putting together a viable policy.

Insurers will normally cost a premium based on their assessment of the level of risk faced by a business. To do this, the insurer will consider the industry sector that the business operates in and review the claims record of the business.

If the business can demonstrate there are rigorous risk management policies in place, and it has a good health and safety record, then the insurer will be more inclined to offer a cheaper premium.

Shop around for the best quotes and weigh up the risks, levels of and cost of the insurance cover.

7. Know Who You Are Dealing With

i. Know your employee

The right employee can help a company grow and build its reputation. However, the opposite can also be true, where having the wrong employee can result in them creating problems in a business. Where employees have access to the internal workings of the business – particularly areas like finance and IT systems – it is important to have a well-structured vetting process in place from day one to carry out thorough background checks and ensure the person is who they say they are.

Most criminal acts by employees are carried out because they are unhappy, feel undervalued or feel the company owes them. They will then justify their act by feeling that it is what they are due. Had they been happy in their employment they may have never considered it, which is also a good reason why it is important to keep employees happy.

ii. Know your customer

For many businesses, bad debt and/or untrustworthy customers are areas where money can be lost. Before dealing with customers and providing them with any credit, it is important to carry out due diligence by doing all the relevant checks to assess the risk and to ensure they haven't been involved in any criminal activity or had any restrictions placed on them. For some businesses this is a legal requirement, for others it is a good practice. However, making sure your customers are who they claim they are is essential for the future of your business. Monitoring customers' credit should be an ongoing process.

iii. Know your supplier

Having an unreliable supplier creates a weak link in any business, which has the potential to damage your business, your own financial stability and reputation. It is of great importance to ensure that no unethical business practices, bribes or criminal activity of any kind are carried out that will reflect badly on your business.

Where access to your finances is being provided to accountants, bookkeepers, legal firms and the like, it is important to always ensure that you retain the ultimate control and never create an opportunity for them to exploit their access rights.

It is important to ensure the same with access to your IT systems and put in place steps to ensure your technology is secure and there is no risk of information leaking. Should an IT company have access to sensitive data, don't be scared to impose additional controls on them.

Always ensure you know:

- Who is accessing your data?
- How do they protect your data?
- How well do they know their staff?
- Are their offices and systems secure?

8. Ensure your technology is secure

Virtually all businesses store information electronically and the loss or leak of information can bring the business to a standstill or cause significant disruption. If the loss includes sensitive data, it can be very damaging and destroy your reputation.

The extent of the business IT infrastructure will depend on the nature, size and requirements of the business.

Lots of systems companies are now using cloud-based services, but is it safe to have your data held anywhere apart from within your own walls? Where this is the case, it is always important to check the terms and conditions and how safe the information is. You may wish to have information stored both internally where you have direct control, and externally with cloud-based services for back-up.

9. Stay up to date with the news and competition in your industry

Having good and reputable news sources can help you stay up to date, safeguard your business and take advantage of opportunities to stay ahead of the competition.

The local, national and international economy can take fast turns now, which can have a fast and dramatic impact. These changes can bring difficult times and big opportunities to the well-informed.

10. Security

Depending on the nature and value of the business goods, you may wish to consider having security measures put in place such as:

- CCTV Equipment.
- Security alarm systems.
- Security entry systems.
- Security guards and/or dogs.
- Safe / vaults.
- Tracking equipment.

- Secure perimeter fencing.

It is always important to weigh up all the risks and take reasonable action to reduce them wherever possible.

It is essential to have the right measures in place to safeguard your business, and protect the wealth you have built up from all your effort and hard work.

CHAPTER 15

SIMPLICITY IS THE ULTIMATE BUSINESS SOPHISTICATION

One of the things that never ceases to amaze me is the lengths that some people will go to in overcomplicating even the simplest of tasks. It's common sense that wisdom is simple sophistication. Yet, so often, people who are otherwise sensible in business and their personal lives, are quick to complicate and add layers of confusion. If something is not working, rather than look at the issue objectively and attempt to simplify matters, the usual method is to add another feature, more "stuff" and more reports thinking that it will be the solution. To see how this works in real life, we just need to have a look at how governmental departments work at local and national levels in comparison to successful private organisations. For example, think of the last experience you had in dealing with a government department and how many steps you had to take in order to get the result you were looking for, in comparison to ordering an item of goods from Amazon.

Over-complication is always one of the key issues that I see in every failure or underperforming company (or individual person for that matter). Avoid those who have a problem for every solution, and seek out those who are committed to finding a simple solution to every problem. As an entrepreneur, this is your primary task and where your greatest opportunities come from.

Simplicity is genius – and the role of genius is to simplify the complicated, which is the key to achieving success. Complexity confuses people and as mentioned previously, "if you confuse them, you lose them." Complexity also undermines confidence and is not just the enemy of execution, but also the enemy of success.

The simpler you can make and keep things, the more understanding and belief your customers and teams will have in your vision. This improves efficiency, effectiveness, productivity, satisfaction and generates the best results. People are not afraid of hard work, but they are afraid of failure. Complexity adds to fear and erodes confidence, which leads to failure.

The simpler we can keep things, the more successful we will be. It's as simple as that!

As a company grows, new levels of complexity tend to creep into the business, and this can happen at every level. This can spread like weeds growing in a garden. All CEOs and executives tend to experience this as a company grows and increases market share, revenues, earnings, number of employees, number of products and/or services offered, etc. Communication also gets harder and "priorities" tend to grow exponentially as each group and department wants to contribute to the company's success, which can often lead to internal issues dominating where the leader's attention gets focused and pulled away from what really matters.

Company owners, executives and managers often recognise the negative impact that complexity has on productivity and morale, and that they need to go through a process of simplification, but admit that they sometimes do not know where to start.

Agreeing that complexity is a problem is one thing, but doing something about it is another. People often feel that they do not have time to do anything about it due to their current workload, which ends up in a Catch-22 situation, where having the problem precludes the ability to solve it.

It's important to have a strategic framework in place where everyone has the time, encouragement and support to focus on and address the process of simplifying complexity.

Here are seven ways to begin:

1. Always start with your customers

The focus of any company should always be making the customer experience easier and more enjoyable. It is always a good idea to step outside the company and place yourself in the position of a customer and consider what the experience of doing business with your company is like. Go through the process of buying every one of your products or services and assess every touchpoint in the customer journey and pressure test every pre-conceived notion about what customers value and what they don't.

The simpler and smoother you can make the process and experience the better. It is the simple brands that win.

Simple brands are characterised by an ability to cut through the clutter and deliver what consumers want, when they want it, in a manner that they like, without hassle. Amazon is a great example of making the customer experience simple and hassle free.

2. The company mission

It's critical that everyone understands and agrees that simplification is a company priority so that the barriers between different departments and groups are eliminated. This requires commitment from the very top that simplicity permeates the entire organisation.

One of the greatest barriers and challenges to simplification is getting different departments, groups and people to work together and leave behind their competing interests to achieve positive outcomes. It is important to engage everyone in the company vision and make them an integral part of it. When employees understand their individual roles in the business, it's much easier to cut through complexities. Try focusing on a small number of extraordinary initiatives, using small teams with clearly-defined responsibilities.

3. Examine everything

Some companies are so focused on customer satisfaction that they forget about the employee experience of working for the company. Making your business more enjoyable to work for by making things easier for your employees, is also another important factor of building a successful company. Whilst a company cannot exist without customers, it is also true that if a business wishes to grow, it cannot exist without employees either. It all begins with having top-down and bottom-up attitude that requires an empathetic and uncompromising approach, with regular reviews of every part of the business. Simplicity is cultivated through empowerment. It's important to invite and encourage input from everyone on everything. As an easy starting point get rid of any stupid rules, low-value activities, timewasters, and troublemakers. When you shed what's not necessary internally, it leads to improving both the internal and external experience and breeds a culture of simplification, which encourages employees to come up with their own ideas to simplify ways of working.

4. Get well organised

Some business owners focus on getting the business organised when they are not organised themselves or get so focused on the business that they end up becoming unorganised. If you're not naturally inclined to stay organised without conscious thought, failing to have strong systems in place can really put you and your business at a disadvantage. Personal organisation is one of the keys to a happy work environment. The more you can do to keep your work life orderly, the easier it will be to simplify your business.

Here are a few of the best ways to help you stay organised:

- **Clean up your desk** – An organised desk is the sign of an organised mind and an organised mind is required to create simple processes.

- **Streamline your hiring** – Always ask specific, direct questions and contact each candidate's previous employers and their referees. Paint the picture of how they will fit into your business culture and existing team. Having the right employees appointed is essential to the smooth running of a company.

- **Re-engineer your meetings** – Keep meetings short and to the point and only have those required present. Always have a clear purpose for the meeting and an agenda and clear action points.

- **Hire PA / administrative support** – Having a PA / admin support can really help keep things organised and allow you to focus on the important tasks and actions.

- **Delegate** – Delegate as much as you can to people who can do the things equally or better than you. Effective delegation frees up your mind to focus on the bigger picture – this is the best viewpoint from which to look at simplification. You can use the Eisenhower matrix mentioned earlier in this book to help you select the tasks to delegate to others.

- **Prioritise, prioritise, prioritise –** One of the keys to simplification is to figure out what's important and what's not and to continually assess the items on the list and what can be added to it, removed and what the priorities are. Work on your important ideas first. The Eisenhower matrix is also a helpful tool to help prioritise.

5. Clarify-Define-Streamline

- **Clarify –** Once you can clarify your purpose – why you do what you do and how you do it – everything becomes a lot simpler. Having a simple, clear company purpose clarifies intent both internally and externally and helps define your path, your products and your place in the market. The key is to never lose sight of that purpose.

- **Define –** Defining what truly matters is important so that everyone in the organisation clearly understands their roles and responsibilities. Complexity has the tendency to add layers of management. When this happens, managers can end up justifying their position by questioning everything their subordinates are doing, which adds to unnecessary confusion and work, creating even further complexity and lowered morale. To reduce this kind of complexity and micromanagement, the flatter and more clearly defined the structure of an organisation is the better. It's also important to define what the company KPIs are so that they can be reviewed and improved.

- **Streamline –** Always be looking at ways to take the shortest path from here to there, without taking shortcuts that compromise the desired outcome. Once it's clear that you are working on the right things, root out the extra steps and people to make the processes as lean as possible. One of the most effective ways to simplify organisational processes is to standardise all recurring and identical processes.

6. Keep everything open to review and change if necessary

In order to truly and effectively simplify things, you need to have the courage to start with a blank page and stop being so nice. One of the habits that causes or exacerbates complexity is not speaking up about poor practices. This is particularly true when employees hesitate to challenge more senior people who unintentionally cause complexity through poor time and meeting management, unclear instructions and assignments, unnecessary emails, poor personal or bad managerial habits. The more you listen to your team, the better the entire group will work. Make a list of things that are not working and can be simplified, and do not hesitate to remove anything that's not working and cannot be improved.

7. Avoid the technology trap

One of the biggest traps that I see people falling into today relates to technology. Everyone wants the latest and greatest tools, but it becomes a vicious cycle to maintain. Every day there are new apps and software being released that promise to help you work more efficiently and save money or streamline your customer communications. What you need to focus on is increasing the use of your existing technology. The chances are, you are only using a fraction of its capabilities. Just because a product or idea is new to you, doesn't mean it's better than what you already have or are already are doing.

When we talk about simplification, we are aiming to reduce the amount of time we spend on something rather than adding to it – a fact we sometimes forget!

Take Action and Stick To The BASICS

- **B**enefit – Does it provide benefit to the customer, employees and the company?
- **A**dvantage – Is it advantageous to the customer, employees and the company?
- **S**tandardisation – Standardise every recurring process to a high standard.
- **I**nvestment – Will it provide a good return on investment of time and money?
- **C**ustomer Satisfaction – Will it lead to greater customer satisfaction?
- **S**imple – Keep everything simple. Is it already simple or is it simple to simplify?

Simplifying your business may seem like a chore, but it doesn't have to be. By committing to keeping your business simple and on the right track, you'll be operating with less stress and more efficiency.

CHAPTER 16

SELLING YOUR BUSINESS

An exit strategy may be the last thing on a business owner's mind, particularly during the start-up phase. Nevertheless, it is important to have an exit strategy in mind right from the beginning. The type of business you choose should depend on your goals, and the way you grow it should be aligned with your exit strategy. Even if your exit strategy is technically your last move, it doesn't matter if you are viewing business ownership as being for five to ten years or if you plan to spend your entire career owning the same business. Most people eventually plan to retire at a certain age, plus it is important to keep in mind that we never know what the future holds, so it is better to build a business that can be sold than one that costs a lot of money to close down. Selling your business could be where the large reward for all your efforts comes from.

I have seen business owners who have been in business for long periods, sometimes 30 years, who would like to have sold their business as a going concern in order to retire. However, they were unable to do so or had to wait another 10 plus years to achieve it. I made the same mistake myself some years ago, when I built up a successful business which I lost interest in. Instead of selling it as a going concern, I held on to it, hoping the passion would come back – only for the business to continue to decline. In the end, I had the costs of closing it down and selling the assets individually. On every occasion I have seen this, it could have been avoided with a better exit strategy and plan.

Exiting your business is inevitable at some point and something that will happen whether you're in control of it or not, so having a good exit strategy plan creates a win-win because it's important to remember that anything that you do to benefit your future buyer, will also benefit you. You'll have a more efficient, profitable business that is easy to manage.

Of all the businesses for sale, it is only around 20% of them that will achieve a sale.

What Is a Business Exit Strategy?

A business exit strategy is a plan for what will happen when you want to leave your business. Just like you have a business plan to guide your business throughout its life, you should also have an exit plan, which could be a separate plan or part of your larger business plan. It might even be a good idea to revisit and review how you feel about your business exit strategy annually at the same time as you review your main business plan. Our life and plans evolve, and it is important to keep our plans up to date.

Many business owners start their business with the express purpose of exiting after a certain number of years. It doesn't mean they are less committed entrepreneurs. It just means they a have a plan in place and clear goal of where they would like to be.

The exit planning starts with determining your personal and business goals, and then assessing your mental and financial readiness. After this, you need to identify the exit options that are most aligned with your goals.

The aim is to have a well thought out exit strategy to leave your business in the best possible shape for a new owner, which can increase the sale price. This means it should be operating at peak profitability, the accounts and records should be up to date, and all your processes will be written down and systemised, so that a stranger can come in and take over at any time. It can take time to build a business that can run entirely without you being there. That's why it's never too soon to start on your succession plan or exit strategy.

What Are The Reasons for Exiting A Business?

There are many reasons to plan a good business exit strategy. They include:

- Planned exit in several years' time.
- Retirement.
- Change in circumstances.
- Change of interests.
- Health issues.
- An unexpected offer is received.

- Wish to follow new or more lucrative venture.
- Need to access money.
- Wanting to spend more time with family.

Leaving at the right time can often be the best decision for both you and your business in the long run. No person or business benefits from having an owner and leader who either can't or doesn't want to invest their time and effort into running it.

The Best Kind of Business Exit Strategy

The best kind of business exit strategy is the one that's right for you and your business and is planned well in advance.

Exit strategies are not about planning for the worst. They are about how you can turn a good situation into a great one. If you only start to think about your exit strategy when your business is in trouble, it is already too late, and you will have a hard time positioning yourself for a soft landing.

9 Business Exit Strategy Plans

1. Legacy – Pass the business along to a family member.
2. Merger and acquisitions (M&A).
3. Pursue an "acquihire".
4. Have existing managers buy you out.
5. Sell your stake to a partner/investor.
6. Plan an initial public offering (IPO).
7. Become a lifestyle entrepreneur.
8. Liquidate the business.
9. File for bankruptcy.

1. **Legacy:** Many entrepreneurs start their business with the desire to create a legacy that they can pass on to their family. This involves creating a plan for transitioning the company to a child or another relative at a certain point in the future. This may seem attractive because you can prepare successors over a period of time. However, it is important to bear in mind that your family may not have the same vision as you and maybe do not want to take

over the business or maybe they are not the best or right people to continue its success.

2. **Mergers and acquisitions:** Your business either merges with another company or gets bought out – this can be a good win-win strategy when other companies have complementary skills and can benefit from economies of scale. For larger companies, it can be a more efficient and quicker way to grow their revenue than creating new products and growing organically. Depending on who you sell to or merge with, it could also provide you with flexibility in terms of whether you continue to stay involved full- or part-time for a period, or you have the freedom to completely walk away. One of the biggest advantages of this exit strategy is the ability to negotiate the selling price.

3. **"Acquihire":** This is where a company buys out a business to acquire the value in its talented and skilled employees. Although this means your legacy may not continue in name, it will help take care of your employees, which is often a business owner's biggest concern. It is important to negotiate with your employees' needs in mind: they came to work for you and showed their loyalty and commitment to you, not another business. I know from personal experience of buying a company mainly to increase my workforce, it can be a difficult time for employees with the uncertainty that comes with change.

4. **Management/employee buyout:** The existing management team and/or employees buy out the business. This can result in a smoother transition and increase loyalty to your business's legacy. It can also allow flexibility in terms of your involvement. They might want to keep you on as a consultant, advisor, mentor, which can be a good thing for both parties, particularly during the early days.

5. **Sell your stake to a partner/investor:** If you aren't the sole owner of the company, you could sell your share to an existing business partner or new investor. This can be a relatively-easy exit strategy, depending on your existing business partner and the new buyer. The advantage is that the business can operate and continue as usual, whilst you can remove yourself completely from the business.

6. **Initial public offering (IPO):** This used to be a lucrative strategy for young ambitious companies or larger companies, and the quick route to riches where the business was prepared and sold to the public. However, since the Internet bubble burst in 2000, the IPO rate has significantly declined and is not seen as the recommended approach today. For an IPO to be successful, the economy and business conditions need to be right – and even if your business is booming, shareholders are demanding and liability concerns are high. This can mean that your industry may not appeal to the public in a way that gets the stock investors excited, which could end up devaluing your company and achieving the opposite result of what was intended. The IPO process can be complex, takes time and is costly. Your business will also come under intense scrutiny from stockholders and analysts and this can end up being a stressful process.

7. **Lifestyle entrepreneur:** This is not really a business exit strategy but if you have a healthy business that you are no longer interested in and are unable to sell, and you want to have the freedom to live the life of a lifestyle entrepreneur, you could appoint a management team to run the business for you. It is hard to find a good team and keep them motivated to run the business when they see you living the life of a lifestyle entrepreneur on the back of their hard work, but it is possible. Even if the profits decline, they may still be enough for the lifestyle that you wish to live.

8. **Liquidate:** Closing your business and selling your assets doesn't have to mean defeat – it is just the end of a chapter. It's a good idea though to explore all other options before taking this route. You might have employees and customers who are relying on you and they might have options that you haven't considered. If you decide to take this route, it is important to remember that you will need to pay off any debts and pay out any shareholders, and you are unlikely to get the most bang for your buck with this option.

9. **Bankruptcy:** No one ever wants to file for bankruptcy, and this should be viewed as a last resort when something goes horribly wrong and there are no alternative options left.

How To Sell A Business

10 Steps To Help Plan And Execute A Business Exit Strategy

1. Pick a target buyer

Your buyer could be:

- Family
- Business partner / investor
- Management buyout
- Employee/s
- New buyer
- Highest bidder

Depending on your target buyer, your priorities will change. For example:

- If it's family, it is important to make everything transparent and fair.
- If you're selling to staff, be prepared for staggered payments. They'll probably start with a deposit and pay you the rest from business income.
- If you sell to the highest bidder, then get all your records in order as otherwise they won't have any idea how you operate, or what sort of money you make.

2. Decide how fast you want out

Some buyers – such as family, staff or even a management buyout – won't necessarily have access to all the cash to buy the business outright straight away. In such cases, you might want or must keep an interest in the business and stay involved to protect your investment. If that's the case, you'll need to negotiate a consulting fee. If you want a clean break, a better option would be to sell it on the open market.

3. Have the business accounts up to date

Smart buyers will ask to see at least two years' worth of financial records. It's important to have your accounts looking good, and if there is anything you can do to improve profitability it is worthwhile doing as soon as possible. You want that upswing to show in your accounts as a sustainable trend rather than as a recent spike.

4. Systemise the business

Write a "how to" manual for your business, so that a stranger could pick up the reins and run everything tomorrow. Record every process, including admin. Make a note of the steps you follow for each of these tasks. While you're at it, write formal job descriptions for employees. Create templates for all tasks that are repeated in your business.

Ensure you have formal (and efficient) processes for getting work done. Who does what, when, and how? Make sure there are protocols to guide all this. Potential buyers will be impressed if some things in your business happen automatically.

5. Make yourself easily replaceable

No one's going to buy your business if it can't survive without you. If you have staff, give them the training and authority they need to succeed. Scale back your involvement. Be less available to customers and clients. Delegate big decisions. Go into work less often.

6. Figure out how to increase the valuation

What are the things that make your business great? Do you have a really outstanding product? Loyal customers? Amazing intellectual property? Find the strengths in your business and grow them, so that they become even more valuable. Similarly, figure out the biggest weaknesses and strengthen them.

You'll need someone from outside the business to provide this assessment. Get your accountant involved. If they don't have the particular skills you need, they may be able to recommend someone who does.

7. Appoint a team of experts to help you

Selling or transitioning out of your business can be a complex process in terms of legal, tax, finance, personal and other factors. It is important to have experts who can help you maximise the rewards, minimise the tax implications and put in place the correct legal procedures to protect your interests.

8. Get a business valuation

You won't know what you'll get for your business until the day it's sold, but you can get a guide valuation. Ask for a professional opinion. Your accountant should be able to introduce you to someone, or you could search for a local business broker. A guideline valuation will help satisfy your curiosity and set realistic expectations. If they predict a lower price than you'd hoped, you might delay your exit and spend some time building value in the business.

9. Have a good sales pitch

Buyers need to be excited by your business, so come up with an elevator pitch that captures the essentials. Craft a story that explains why you got started, how you've grown, and what you've achieved. Paint a positive picture of the future too, but keep it real. Incorporate statistics and facts to support what you're saying.

10. Exit strategy completed

Completing the exit out of your business can come with a wide range of mixed and, quite often, strong emotions. The transition can be a difficult time for some. It is important that you have a life plan after the business exit is complete. This might be: seeking out a new adventure; starting a new business; retiring and taking life easy; travelling; spending more time with family; contributing to society; or just having the freedom to choose each day. Everyone has the human desire for growth and contribution. The moment we stop growing is the moment we start slowly dying. When we are contributing in some way, we feel a part of society – this comes with big rewards for others, but also to ourselves.

CHAPTER 17

SUCCESS MINDSET

Self-made wealthy individuals, millionaires and billionaires, think, speak and act differently to those who are poor or stuck in a lower- or middle-income range. Much of how you look at the world and your results will depend on your childhood and upbringing. The good news is that it is possible to change whatever limiting beliefs and unhealthy habits that you have, which are holding you back from achieving the level of success and results that you would like to achieve. It all starts with taking full accountability and responsibility for your own life.

In order to achieve the level of financial independence and freedom that you have been dreaming about, it is essential to develop and adopt a 'success mindset' and tune in to your intuition. Without it, you will remain stuck where you are, going around in circles and remaining in the same position. We cannot expect to achieve a different result if we keep repeating the same actions.

Most people who look at the lives of those who are successful, underestimate the value of talent, work ethic and mindset in their successes, and overestimate the value of luck. There is no such thing as good or bad luck. We make our own luck. Life is always happening for us, not to us.

> *"When we change the way we look at things and our view of*
> *the world, the things we look at and*
> *the world around us changes."*
> **– Calum Kirkness**

In order to achieve success, it is essential to take 100% responsibility for your own life and drop any victim mentality. I am sure that one of the reasons you are looking to get in to business (and if you are already in business) is to create the time and financial freedom to live life on your terms and build wealth?

Like anything in life, there are strategies to create wealth and live the life you want.

Strategies For Building Wealth

In many ways, owning a business is a metaphor for life: it's a balancing act that requires resilience, knowledge and skill to stay afloat. If you are already in business, you may be wondering if simply making a profit is a worthy enough goal and rather than just surviving, you are most likely craving abundance and the sense of security that it provides to give you the freedom to live life on your own terms. Building wealth is key to creating prosperity, but many people struggle with creating it due to misconceptions about the process. The good news is that with the right mindset and strategies in place, you can master the process of elevating your business, your wealth and your life to the next level.

Building Wealth Is About More Than Just Money

Money is merely a vehicle to carry you to financial freedom. With financial freedom in place, you can then pursue your dreams and find lasting happiness and fulfilment. In order to enjoy the money that you have made, it is equally important that you enjoyed how you made it. If you were miserable and required constant motivation to achieve financial freedom, the chances are that you won't enjoy it and will end up self-sabotaging it.

How To Build Wealth And Keep It

The second step in building wealth is aligning your financial decisions with your passions by building your deepest values into your approach. To discover your deepest values, you can ask yourself these questions:

- What do I want most out of life?
- What is missing in my life?
- What are my biggest fears?
- What inspires me?
- What do I feel is impossible?
- What do I want for the people I love?

Once you get in touch with your deepest value system, you can align your spending priorities and Incorporate them into a budget that you can then track and hold yourself accountable for living below your means. Once you've developed a baseline of financial freedom, you must put your wealth to work by investing it wisely.

Overcoming Emotional Spending To Retain Your Wealth

A critical component in building wealth is keeping the wealth that you create. This requires making mindful decisions about how you invest and spend your money. Instead of letting emotional spending derail the process, it is important that you learn to control your emotions. By developing strategies to manage your emotions, you will become aware of how your feelings are influencing your financial decisions and be better placed to make better and deliberate spending choices.

As you tap into your inner creativity while sticking to your financial strategy, you'll become more confident in your ability to manage your finances. The resultant cycle creates upward momentum in learning how to build wealth effectively; you increase your self-efficacy, which in turn allows you to build more wealth.

Many wealthy people and self-made millionaires drive used cars, live in average neighbourhoods, wear average-priced clothes, watches and accessories and are very careful with their money. If you follow some of the rich and famous, you will be able to see that this is the case. There is a big difference between those who are rich and those who *look* rich!

> *"The object of the game is to be rich and happy, not look rich,*
> *but broke and unhappy."*
> **– Calum Kirkness**

Your job is to learn and adopt the knowledge and habits of a success mindset and become one of those people who are genuinely rich. Anyone can become rich with the right mindset.

In order to understand the difference between a wealthy and poor mindset, there are a few key differences.

Those who are successful understand:

- The difference between assets and liabilities. Assets produce an income and/or increase in value over time. Liabilities cost money and/or decrease in value over time.
- The effects of leveraging their time and money, and when and how to use it for maximum effect.
- The power of the compound effect.
- That everything is energy. Positive thoughts exude positive emotions, which attract positive people, opportunities and outcomes.
- The importance of the people they surround themselves with. Positive people encourage growth and are happy for other people's success, whereas negative people have a problem for everything and feel jealous or resentful to see others succeeding.
- The importance of their environment and the places they spend time in. Our environment has a big impact on our wellbeing and success. Being in a natural or positive environment is beneficial to the results that you can achieve.
- How our minds work. We are not our thoughts and we can control how much attention we give to them.
- That time is our most precious commodity and valuable asset, and therefore understand the importance of how to manage it.

Another important wealth factor to understand and assess is your current financial comfort zone. Think of it in the same way as how the central heating system in your house operates, where the thermostat will come on when the temperature becomes too low and/or will switch off when the temperature gets too high. The same is true with your level of wealth thermostat (comfort zone around money).

When you feel uncomfortable with having too little money in your bank account or too much debt, you will start to save until the level gets back within your financial comfort zone. When you have more money or wealth than you are comfortable with, you will spend some money until your bank balance falls back into your financial comfort zone. You might not even have been aware of this until someone highlights it to you, as it is usually all happening without your conscious awareness. It is the reason why so many lottery winners end up back where they were before their won.

Work on developing a success mindset by retraining or reprogramming your subconscious mind – removing negative attitudes and limiting beliefs towards money and wealth, and learning how to tap into and listen to your intuition. If you don't, you will remain stuck where you are – running off course, feeling frustrated and knowing that you have more to give, but unable to identify what this is.

How To Develop A Success Mindset

Let's look at how you can learn the secrets of the millionaire mind and what steps you need to take for it to become your reality.

Replacing limiting beliefs with positive ones

First, you must identify your limiting beliefs around money in order to release them.

Some common and typical limiting beliefs are:

- Money is the root of all evil.
- Money doesn't grow on trees.
- You must have money to make money.
- You must work hard to make a lot of money.
- You can't buy happiness.
- The more money you have, the more problems you have.
- I don't have what it takes to make a lot of money.
- I can make money, but I can't seem to hold on to it.
- Money is not that important: it's only money.
- Money is there to be spent.
- The rich get richer and the poor get poorer.
- I'm just not good with money.
- My family has never been rich.

If you are to become financially free and build wealth for your freedom and security, it is essential for you to replace any limiting beliefs and develop a success mindset. Money on its own is not bad. It is the interpretation and use of it by some people that can make it appear bad. The opposite is true, and it can be used for a lot of good.

When we look at the behaviour and approach of those who are financially successful and those who struggle to create wealth, there are several key differences.

Comparison Of A Successful Mindset vs. An Unsuccessful Mindset:

Success Mindset (Growth Mindset)	Unsuccessful Mindset (Fixed Mindset)
Abundant mindset	Scarcity mindset
Embraces change	Fears change
Wants others to succeed	Secretly hopes others fail
Manages time well	Always busy but unproductive
Accepts responsibility for failures	Blames others
Exudes joy	Exudes anger
Talks about ideas	Talks about people
Shares information	Hoards information
Gives credit to others	Takes all the credit
Sets goals	Doesn't set goals
Writes down their plans	Has no plans
Keeps a journal	Doesn't keep a journal
Reads books	Watches TV
Transformational perspective	Transactional perspective
Continuously learning	Thinks they know it all already
Compliments others	Criticises others
Forgives others	Holds grudges
Has gratitude	Has a sense of entitlement
Associates with positive people	Associates with negative people
Patient	Impatient

Developing a success mindset takes time and patience and requires an open mind.

In most cases, people become wealthy over a long period of time. It is usually based on slow, incremental growth in the beginning, which speeds up, resulting from smart use of leveraging as the compound effect builds momentum.

The next time you think that an action is too small to be taken or a goal is too far away to achieve, think about the compound effect.

Below are some examples of the power of the compound effect:

£10 to £1 Million in One Round of Golf!

Imagine you are out for a round of golf with your friend and to add a little extra competition and spice to the match, you agree to play for some money. The rule is that you will start and play the first hole for £10. Then, each hole you play, the money doubles.

Hole 1 = £10
Hole 2 = £20
Hole 3 = £40
Hole 4 = £80
Hole 5 = £160
Hole 6 = £320
Hole 7 = £640
Hole 8 = £1,280
Hole 9 = £2,560
Hole 10 = £5,120
Hole 11 = £10,240
Hole 12 = £20,480
Hole 13 = £40,960
Hole 14 = £81,920
Hole 15 = £163,840
Hole 16 = £327,680
Hole 17 = £655,360
Hole 18 = £1,310,720

You can see the incredible power of understanding the compound effect and having it work in your favour. One small action today, repeated consistently and frequently, can build momentum and have a great effect.

When you borrow money to buy liabilities (bad debt), that is the compound effect working in reverse against you. It's like starting at the 18th hole and working your way back to the 1st.

One Pence To £10 Million In Under One Month!

Another example that illustrates the power of the compound effect is: if you take 1p today and double it each day, you will be a millionaire on day 21, and in 31 days you would have £1,073,741,824. That rate of growth and doubling every day would be very hard to achieve. But even a small percentage difference in the discount that you can negotiate in deals, and the greater efficiency and growth that you can achieve, all compounds over time into making a big difference in increasing profits and wealth.

Day 1	£1.00
Day 2	£2.00
Day 3	£4.00
Day 4	£8.00
Day 5	£16.00
Day 6	£32.00
Day 7	£64.00
Day 8	£128.00
Day 9	£256.00
Day 10	£512.00
Day 11	£1,024.00
Day 12	£2,048.00
Day 1	£4,096.00
Day 14	£8,192.00
Day 15	£16,384.00
Day 16	£32,768.00
Day 17	£65,536.00
Day 18	£131,072.00
Day 19	£262,144.00
Day 20	£524,288.00
Day 21	**£1,048,576.00**
Day 22	£2,097,152.00

Day 23	£4,194,304.00
Day 24	£8,388,608.00
Day 25	£16,777,216.00
Day 26	£33,554,432.00
Day 27	£67,108,864.00
Day 28	£134,217,728.00
Day 29	£268,435,456.00
Day 30	£536,870,912.00
Day 31	**£1,073,741,824.00**

The Snowball Effect

You may have heard the compound effect described as the snowball effect. The snowball effect is a metaphor for compounding, and it demonstrates how small actions repeated over time can lead to big results. When you make a snowball in your hands and start rolling it down a hill, with each revolution the snowball gathers more and more snow, and by the time it reaches the bottom of the hill it has grown into a large snow boulder.

Success Mindset Rules:

- Develop the habits and mindset of successful and wealthy people.
- Trust and follow your intuition.
- Focus on achieving and getting what you want.
- Become goal-oriented.
- Don't worry about the competition – winners focus on winning; losers focus on winners.
- Look at ways to increase your knowledge – the best investment that you can ever make is in yourself.
- Look at ways to increase your income without losing any time.
- Don't spend your money – carefully consider every expenditure. Remember the power of saving a little each day and the compound effect can work in both directions.
- Save and invest your money – stop working for your money (selling your time for money) and make your money work for you.
- Be patient – never allow yourself to feel that a financial investment decision is urgent and must be made immediately.

- Due diligence – the wealthy understand the importance of due diligence and the value of getting expert advice.
- Think big – start off with small goals and use your success mindset, leverage, and the compound effect to achieve big results.
- Take responsibility for your future – push hard enough for anything and you will achieve your goals.
- Safeguard and protect your assets – as you begin to accumulate money and assets, adopt a wealthy habit of protecting them.

Our entire life is largely determined by just a few things:

- What we do – employee, self-employed, business owner, investor. We tend to either follow our intuition or follow our programming.
- Who we choose to do it with – spouse, work colleagues, business partners, friends.
- Who we do it for – boss, customers, friends, community, all of society.
- Why we do it – is it for you, others, and/or both?
- Where we do it – the places where you live, work, visit.
- Spending / investment habits – are you a spender, saver, investor?

I don't know about you, but for me, having the freedom to choose is what I want. I want to be able to choose:

- What work I do.
- Who I work with.
- Where I work.
- Why I work.
- My income levels.
- How I spend, save and invest.
- Being able to help other people.

Success is generally all about doing the opposite to the masses. The current mainstream model is broken, where we are programmed with limiting beliefs and fears from our parents because they don't know any better and think that they are protecting us. The education system is designed to turn children into employees: the employment system turns us into slaves who build other people's dreams rather than our own; the government takes away our freedom, to retain control over us; the mainstream media works for the government and establishment, and programmes us with the content to that the establishment wishes to push; the financial sector is designed to rob the poor; the medical sector treats symptoms rather than causes in order that we become long-term customers.

Do not take advice from anyone who hasn't done what you would like to do, and be careful when taking advice from second-generation wealth.

There will be people on your journey who will try to hold you back; you will have haters as you make progress on your journey to success. As you grow, others will become jealous and some might try to pull you back. Look on jealousy and hate from others as a sign that you are growing and going in the right direction. No one ever hated anyone who was behind them.

If anyone takes up space in your mind with negative thoughts, evict them immediately. If they refuse to leave, increase the rent immediately until they can no longer afford to live there!

> *"Life is magical, not logical. If your dreams are logical,*
> *they are not big enough. Dream big and when you believe in*
> *yourself and believe in your dreams,*
> *the magic will start to happen."*
> **– Calum Kirkness**

It is also important how we talk to ourselves and others. Words have incredible power, which influence the results that you achieve. Here is a list of your likely chances of success based on some of the thoughts and words that you may say to yourself and others:

- I won't – 0%
- I can't – 10%
- I don't know – 20%
- I wish I could – 30%
- I want to – 40%
- I think I might – 50%

- I might – 60%
- I think I can – 70%
- I can – 80%
- I am – 90%
- I did – 100%

Everyone wakes up one day and realises that time is running out for the things that they would like to do. You only live once but if you do it right, once is enough. The good news is that it is never too late to start.

Time Is Our Most Precious Commodity And Valuable Asset

Rich or poor, we are all given the same amount of time each day. It is how we use the time that we are given that counts.

Time is our most valuable commodity and precious asset and we all wake up each morning with 86,400 seconds in our time account. Never complain that you are poor, think of those 86,400 seconds in your time account (which is the same amount as all the billionaires have), and invest this time in things that matter. You cannot roll these seconds forward to another day. The actions that you take today create your tomorrow.

Imagine if someone stole £100 or even £10 from you, you would be disappointed and go after them. But what about the people who are stealing your time by focusing on negativity and drama that is not serving you. The next time someone is stealing your time, think about it as them taking £1 from your time account for every one second you spend with them.

We will all hear negatives things said to us and about us. It can only take 10 seconds to hear or read a comment that can destroy our day, week or even occupy our time for a longer period. View the comment that takes 10 seconds to hear as someone taking £10 from your time account and don't give them a penny more. Instead, switch back to the thought of how you are going to spend those valuable seconds now. How you spend your time today is what creates your tomorrow.

*"Invest your time wisely today in order to
have a better tomorrow."*
– Calum Kirkness

The most important part of the process in developing a success mindset is the person that you must become in terms of courage, character, thoughtfulness and persistence in building your business and creating your dream life. Anyone can become a successful entrepreneur. It is never the lack of resources that prevents anyone from starting. It is the lack of resourcefulness.

What Now?

Your dreams and ideas won't come screaming at you head on or tell you this is what you must do or who you must become. Our intuition softly and gently whispers to us and guides us on the right path, but it can be hard to hear the message the way that we live our lives today. When we carefully tune in and listen to what our intuition is telling us, the strongest message comes from how it makes us feel. If your idea tickles your heart, it's a sure sign that you are on the right path. Not only will you benefit from following it, but everyone that you meet and serve along the journey will also benefit.

I believe that we are all born to be the greatest at something and when we find our natural strengths, talents and passions, it is very hard for others to compete with us on them.

Everything you need to create the life that you desire already exists inside you, but we sometimes need a little guidance, inspiration and support to bring everything out and put it all together.

You are clearly someone with ambition and a desire to build a successful business as you are reading this book, and I would encourage you to believe in yourself and your dreams.

If you are ready to unleash your genius, you can use your natural strengths, talents and passions to build your dream business. You can turn your passions into profit and fulfil your purpose by making a contribution and difference in the world. However, you must *take action* in order to achieve your goals and dreams.

Once you start on your business journey, it is important to have the right support to help you stay on track and keep the forward momentum going until you become unstoppable.

If you are waiting for the right time, it is now. You don't have to be great or have everything ready to start, but you must start in order to become great.

If you would like some help and support in assessing your ideas and setting up, systemising and scaling your business, Business Success Insider is here to help you.

Coaching and mentoring is a way of life – it's all about how we can get more out of a shorter period of time. We all have so many demands placed on us in today's fast-paced world that unless there is someone there to help us control and measure our focus, then we usually don't maximise things to the level that we could. Mentoring and coaching is the best way to move towards mastery. If you want the biggest and best results in the shortest period of time, coaching and mentoring is the best option.

There are generally three types of people. The type that you are will dictate whether you succeed or not, what level of success you are likely to achieve in your business, and the quality of life that you are likely to live:

- **The Dabbler Character – Has Desire But No Determination and No Coach**
  The dabbler starts and improves, but soon afterwards reaches a plateau. They continue for a little while but give up easily after seeing no further quick growth, believing that it is not for them. They then try something else and repeat the same cycle.

  For a dabbler to break through and achieve new improved results, it is important for them to have a coach or mentor at each stage who can help them up to the next level.

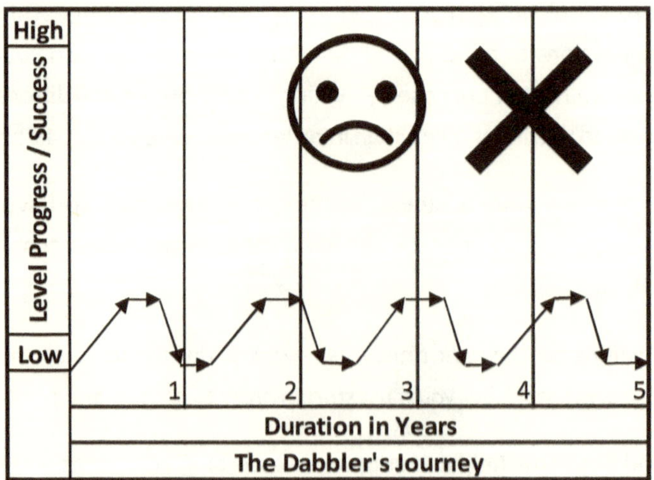

- **The Stresser Character – Has Desire and Determination but No Coach**

   The stresser has the desire and the determination, but persists on their own without a coach. They push through the plateaus and get breakthroughs, but get burnt out. It takes them a long time to reach significantly high skill and result levels.

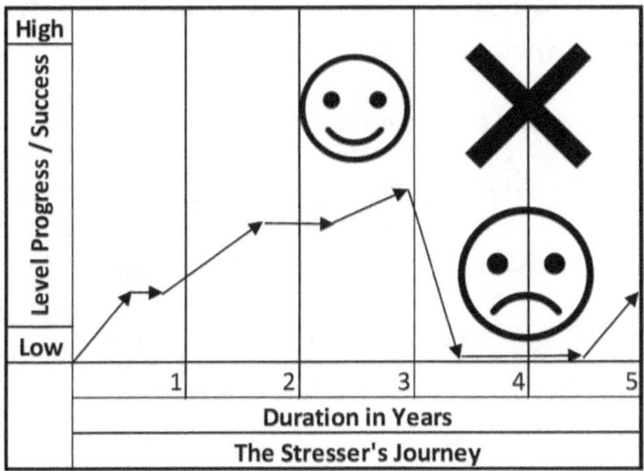

- **The Master Character – Has Desire, Has Determination and Has Coach or Mentor**

   The master knows that they are going to hit challenges along the way and plateau at times, but rather than struggle for the next breakthrough they know that each time they hit one they need to find the right coach to continue to take them to the next level.

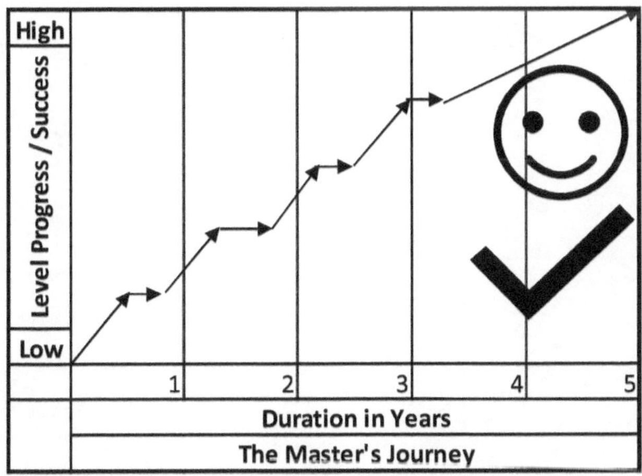

If you wish to become a master of your own success and destiny, contact Business Success Insider today.

At **Business Success Insider**, we run business training events, masterminds, coaching and mentoring programmes and international retreats. Visit www.calumkirkness.com for further details.

You can connect and contact me on:

LinkedIn: Calum Kirkness and Business Success Insider

Facebook: Calum Kirkness and Business Success Insider

Instagram: Calum Kirkness and Business Success Insider

I hope you enjoyed reading this book and
got lots of value from it.

Whichever route you take, I wish you a successful, happy, healthy and abundant life and thank you for taking the time to read this book.

**Please share a review on Amazon to support and
help other readers.**